TRAVELLERS

THE GAMBIA

By
LINDSAY BENNETT

Written by Lindsay Bennett

Original photography by Pete Bennett

Editing and page layout by Cambridge Publishing Management Ltd,
Unit 2, Burr Elm Court, Caldecote CB23 7NU
Series Editor: Karen Beaulah

Published by Thomas Cook Publishing
A division of Thomas Cook Tour Operations Ltd
Company Registration No. 1450464 England

PO Box 227, The Thomas Cook Business Park,
Coningsby Road, Peterborough PE3 8SB, United Kingdom
E-mail: books@thomascook.com
www.thomascookpublishing.com
Tel: +44 (0)1733 416477

ISBN: 978-184157-694-7

Text © 2007 Thomas Cook Publishing
Maps © 2007 Thomas Cook Publishing

Project Editor: Rebecca Snelling
Production/DTP Editor: Steven Collins

Printed and bound in Italy by: Printer Trento.

Front cover credits, L–R: © Thomas Cook; © Jack Sullivan/Alamy;
© Thomas Cook
Back cover credits, L–R: © Thomas Cook; © Thomas Cook

Contents

Introduction

This tiny sliver of a country, cutting a rapier-like plunge into the heart of West Africa, is inextricably bound to the meandering course of the mighty River Gambia. On a continent riven with civil war, famine and social strife, The Gambia is a beacon; a land of relative plenty, of social cohesion and of harmony.

Each of the several ethnic groups living in the country has contributed to a fascinating culture that sustains a population of over one million, from tribal elders to the youngest in the family. The fabric of society is cemented by rites and rituals governing all aspects of life, offering the visitor a window into a totally different world.

Gambians are known for their friendliness; it's easy to see why the brochures call it 'The Smiling Coast'. There's a genuine *joie de vivre* here despite the fact that many live in poverty. It's apparent in the giggling kids and the exuberant adults. Everyone's curious to learn all about strangers in their midst – sometimes to the disquiet of more conservative foreigners.

So much about the country is an enigma, wrapped up in a puzzle, wrapped up in a conundrum. On the one hand a simple agrarian society, yet on the other one of the most vibrant and mature tourist industries on the continent. Roads that don't work, yet an international airport with a runway used as a backup by NASA should they have problems with bringing the space shuttle down safely. It's what makes a visit so interesting; the more you see of the country the less easy it is to pigeonhole it.

The Gambia has always sold itself as a winter sun destination, offering good value R&R in Western-style resorts with sandy beaches, swaying palms, swimming pools and a smiling waiter to deliver a cooling cocktail. And for visitors who simply want a relaxing holiday it certainly delivers, with an added touch of spice missing in most bland concrete Euro-resorts. The journey time from Western Europe is only six hours and The Gambia operates on GMT (the same time as the UK and only one hour behind Ireland and Central Europe), so no jet lag.

But as interest in ecotourism grows, the country is going to attract a whole new generation of fans. Much of the interior remains pristine wilderness, a mixture of mangrove, savannah and deciduous forest that's home to important populations of plants and animals. It's already a top-rated destination for birdwatching and its reputation is bound to grow with the opening of several luxury lodges offering a range of quality sustainable experiences.

For travellers who have never visited sub-Saharan Africa before, The Gambia offers a gentle introduction to this most fascinating region. Here you've got the possibility to test the waters of serious, dirt in your boots, 'get away from it all' itineraries, but with the chance of heading back to an air-conditioned hotel and a well-earned gin and tonic at the end of the day if you find the 'Mungo Park' experience a little too much.

One trip could be the start of a whole new love affair.

A local woman in the Makasuto Cultural Forest

The land

The Republic of The Gambia is continental Africa's smallest country, but don't let the diminutive size fool you into thinking the land has little to offer. The geography is more varied than many of its continental peers, with a wide range of natural ecosystems and a diverse array of flora and fauna to enjoy. The country has several internationally important protected areas, which stand it in good stead as interest in ecotourism grows.

The country

At 11,295sq km (4,360sq miles), The Gambia is twice the size of Wales or slightly less than twice the size of the state of Delaware, but 1,300sq km (502sq miles) of this area is river, so the land mass is technically around 10,000sq km (3,860sq miles). The current borders were drawn up in 1889, agreed between the colonial powers Britain and France, giving the then British colony of Gambia a narrow stretch of territory on either bank of the river running 300km (186 miles) inland from the west coast of Africa. The country benefits from 80km (50 miles) of coastline but inland is only 48km (30 miles) wide at its fullest point, while in the east where the river is narrowest, this drops to around 15km (9 miles) wide, barely wide enough to register on maps of the continent. The 1889 agreement gave Gambia 740km (460 miles) of land borders, all of which are bounded by Senegal. In many ways the easiest explanation of the physical relationship between the two countries is that The Gambia is the meat layer in a Senegal sandwich.

The Gambia is a very flat land. The highest point in the country only reaches 53m (174ft) above sea level, though the river banks do include dramatic sand and laterite 'cliffs' which make impressive vantage points. Laterites are rocks with relatively high concentrations of iron and aluminium caused by the leaching effect of centuries of hard rain, and the resulting rock – a deep red-brown in colour – is used for bricks and for road surfaces where asphalt is in short supply.

The river

The River Gambia is one of Africa's great waterways. Rising some 1,130km (702 miles) inland in what is now the country of Guinea, the water journeys relentlessly westwards, crossing the border into The Gambia 480km (298 miles) from its mouth.

Navigable for almost 600km (373 miles), the river was a useful conduit for early adventurers who could forge their way in dugout canoes into the heart of the then unexplored continent. One fascinating element in the story of the river is its tidal reach, with the rhythmical rise and fall affecting over 520km (323 miles) of its length and saltwater intrusion reaching 200km (124 miles) inland. This tidal reach has always hindered human utilisation of the river banks. The salt inundation makes the soil unusable for growing crops and tides prohibited settlement of the banks – usually villages, even fishing villages, are built some way from the water's edge.

Dense stands of mangroves extend on both sides of the river for over 160km (99 miles), with saltwater mangroves giving way to freshwater mangroves and deciduous forest the further east you travel. The mangrove is cut by hundreds of smaller inlets, called *bolongs*, that constitute an important ecosystem for wildlife.

Where the river once aided travel and navigation, today it hinders smooth travel around the country. The Gambia relies on a few slow and overworked ferries to get from north to south, methods which are becoming ever more outdated and inadequate.

The coast

The Gambia's 80km (50 miles) of coastline constitute some of Africa's westernmost landmass. Hundreds of square kilometres of mangrove protect the land from the, sometimes, violent Atlantic storms and act as a haven for birdlife both native and visiting. However, mangrove gives way to long swathes of sand on other stretches of the coast; beautiful beaches that have helped in the development of the tourist industry. The beaches are, however, one of The Gambia's most fragile environments, prone to being washed away by strong offshore currents and the aforesaid storms.

Land use

Only 27 per cent of The Gambia's land is suitable for farming, though this could be improved if irrigation systems were more widespread. Seventy

PRACTICAL PLANTS

Gambians still live in close harmony with their land and have learned to utilise many trees and plants in the household.

The baobab is very useful. Gambians eat the fruit and pounded leaves are mixed with couscous to make it more digestible. The flesh of the fruit is soaked in water and the liquid is used to relieve bowel pain.

The leaves of the neem tree are boiled and the juice is used to treat the symptoms of malaria. Pounded leaves are added to soap and used to kill hair lice.

Rice husks are a natural irritant to termites. Stinking pea is pounded into powder and used as an insecticide and rodent poison. Sodom apple leaves drive rodents away. Cassia leaves added to linen stores protect textiles from cockroaches and termites. Strip the bark of the grey plum tree and soak it in water for a natural non-fizzy cola.

five per cent of the population still makes a living from the land, so improvements in water use will directly affect the livelihoods of almost a million people. Groundnuts or peanuts are the major crop, but others include rice, millet, sesame, cassava (tapioca) and palm kernels.

Regular flooding of upland plateau areas during the rainy season makes them ideal for growing crops, though the highest plateau areas only a few metres above this band are too dry. Rainfall has fallen 30 per cent in the last 20 years, making increased desertification a major concern. Villages tend to be located in the band between the tidal flows of the river and the land irrigated by the summer rains, meaning women and children must walk daily to tend and harvest the crops.

Almost 30 per cent of the land is classed as woodland and forest, though this percentage is dropping. The major deciduous hardwoods including mahogany and ebony are now prized worldwide, so the government has introduced legislation to protect the last remaining areas and farmers must replant young trees if they wish to harvest mature specimens.

Around the forests and farmland are vast tracts of savannah grasslands, covered in *Pennisetum purpureum* or elephant grass which can reach 4.5m (15ft) in height and which Gambians cut for thatch and fencing. The mighty baobab is the king of the savannah, punctuating the skyline; other leviathans include the silk cottonwood, or kapok, tree and the acacia.

Tending crops in Busumbale

History

c 800 BC The earliest settlers, thought to be ancestors of the present-day Jola, arrive in the region.

c AD 500 Gambia falls under the influence of the Kingdom of Ghana.

c 1000 Senegambia is converted to Islam.

c 1400 The Mandinka rule the Senegambia region from their kingdom in Mali.

1447 Portuguese explorer Nuno Tristão ventures into the River Gambia.

1457 A Portuguese delegation establishes a trading post on St Andrew's Island (now James Island).

1588 The Portuguese sell trade rights on the Gambia River to the British.

1618 King James of England and Scotland grants a charter to a British company to set up trading posts.

1651 The Duchy of Courland (*see p12*) establishes a trading post on the river.

1661 The Duchy of Courland loses control of the trading post due to war in northern Europe.

1783 The Treaty of Paris gives Great Britain possession of Gambia with the French retaining Albreda on the north bank.

1807 Parliament in London bans slavery throughout the British Empire.

1816 Bathurst is established in the mouth of the River Gambia.

1816–88 Gambia is controlled by the British Governor General based in Sierra Leone.

1857 Albreda is ceded to the British.

1888 Gambian territory becomes a separate colonial entity ruled from Bathurst.

1889 France accepts the established borders of Gambia and the territory is declared a British Crown Colony.

1939–45	Gambia becomes an important staging post for naval convoys around the Cape of Good Hope and air convoys run by the US Army Air Corps. As a French colony, surrounding Senegal was considered enemy territory, so Gambia was on a constant state of high alert.
1962	General elections held.
1963	Gambia becomes self-governing.
1965	Gambia becomes independent on 18 February. It joins the Commonwealth of Nations as a constitutional monarchy.
1970	Gambia becomes a republic within the Commonwealth and Sir Dawda Kairaba Jawara becomes head of state.
1973	Bathurst becomes Banjul.
1982	The Senegambia Confederation between Senegal and Gambia is announced. Under the agreement the two countries aim to unify their economies and defence structures.
1989	Gambia withdraws from the Senegambia Confederation.
1994	On 22 July Jawara is toppled in a military coup organised by the Armed Forces Provisional Ruling Council. Lieutenant Yahya A J J Jammeh becomes head of state.
1996	Elections vote Jammeh as President of the newly constituted Republic of The Gambia.
2001	Jammeh is re-elected.
2004	Deyda Hydara, a leading journalist opposed to President Jammeh, is assassinated.
2006	In March a military coup plot is uncovered and the army chief flees the country. Jammeh is re-elected for a third term in September.
2009	The Gambia intends to join the West African Monetary Zone with Ghana, Nigeria, Sierra Leone and Liberia.

The Latvian connection – a short history of the Duchy of Courland

This small corner of the Baltic was for many generations alive with territorial machinations, but the rise of the Duchy of Courland is its most fascinating story. It's a tale of one family with a nose for business set against the backdrop of friction between second-millennium political powerbrokers.

The Duchy was born out of the death throws of the Livonia Confederation and occupied a tract of land west of the Daugava River to the Baltic coast, now part of modern

Cannons by the jetty on James Island (formerly St Andrew's Island)

Latvia. Courland was one of a handful of minor duchies over which Sweden and Poland vied for control.

Gottard Kettler (1561–87), last Master of the Order of Livonia, became the first Duke of Courland in 1516, and he was followed by his sons. Under the early Kettlers, mining and shipbuilding became big business. However, it was the era of Jacob Kettler (1642–82) that brought the Duchy to international attention. At its peak it was less a geographical entity than one of the world's first 'corporations', and Jacob was the Richard Branson or Donald Trump of his day.

He travelled extensively in Europe, extending trading ties. One of the Duchy's major industries was gunpowder, a vital resource for colonial powers, and Courland sold to the major players – Britain, France, Portugal. Jacob built his own trading fleet, and as a mercantile sea-power he took a step into the 'big league' in 1651, founding the colony of St Andrew's Island in the River Gambia where he built Fort Jacob. In 1652 Jacob founded a second overseas colony on Tobago in the West Indies from where he began to trade sugar, tobacco and coffee.

Unfortunately, all this activity and increased wealth caught the attention of both the Poles and the Swedes. In 1655, the Swedes invaded Courland and the Poles came to defend the territory, starting the Swedish–Polish War (1655–60). Jacob was taken prisoner, and his fleet and most of the Duchy's industrial base was destroyed.

The Duchy never really recovered from this conflict, with Jacob's son Friedrich Casimir skimming off the profits to fund a glamorous court. When he died in 1698 his successor Friedrich Wilhelm was only six years old and was controlled by a Polish regent. As a Polish ally, the Duchy was drawn into conflict again with Sweden, and the growing Russian Empire, during the Northern War (1700–21). Later, Friedrich Wilhelm made the astute move of aligning himself to Peter the Great by marrying into the Russian royal family. Unfortunately, on the journey back from his wedding at St Petersburg he became sick and died, and the Kettlers lost control of their Duchy.

Friedrich Wilhelm left a vacuum behind with both Poland and Russia backing rival claimants. At one time there were two Dukes of Courland, but Ernst Biron, backed by Russian ruler Catherine the Great, won through. Biron handed over control of the territory to his son Peter in 1769, but by this time Russia and Poland were entering a period of protracted friction and Peter was happy to absorb his territory into the greater Russia in 1795, signalling the end of the Duchy of Courland.

Fort James (Jacob) ruins

Politics

Politics in The Gambia have been dominated by one larger-than-life character since the mid-1990s. After winning a third term in office in late 2006, President Yahya Abdul-Aziz Jemus Junkung Jammeh has plans to turn his country into an oil-rich, self-sufficient state, despite the fact that not a drop of the black stuff has ever been extracted from Gambian territory.

Jammeh was born on 25 May 1965 and joined the former National Gendarmerie in 1984 after passing several 'O' levels at Gambia High School. He rose through the ranks, taking on high-profile roles in personal surveillance and the security of politicians and visiting dignitaries, reaching the rank of Lieutenant before the military coup that ousted the democratically elected government of Dawda Jawara in 1994. As Chairman of the Armed Forces Provisional Ruling Council who organised the coup, he took control of the country in the immediate aftermath, then retired from the military to take up life as a politician.

Jammeh has pretty much ruled single-handedly since then. After the coup, all political parties with strong ties to the previous Jawara regime were banned, so Jammeh's Alliance for Patriotic Reorientation and Construction won the first election under the new constitution. The parties

were reinstated in 2001, but by this time Jammeh had strong control over the media and a high profile across the country.

Since then, Jammeh's grip on power has tightened and a cult of personality has begun to overshadow party politics. Several sets of new media laws since the

The Gambian flag

The National Assembly building in Banjul

turn of the millennium have restricted freedom of the press even further. In 2004 these new laws allowed the government to imprison journalists found guilty of libel and sedition. Vocal opponent of the legislation and newspaper proprietor Deyda Hydara was shot dead only days after the law came into force.

In 2005 three leading opposition politicians were arrested as part of an undercover operation looking into threats against the regime, and in March 2006, 27 Gambians including top army officers and government officials were arrested for planning to topple the President. A number escaped into neighbouring Senegal, whose government Jemmah accuses of trying to undermine his regime.

There has been tension between the governments of The Gambia and Senegal on and off since the Senegambia Confederation crumbled in 1989. Senegal is desperate to see a bridge built across the River Gambia, to improve communications between Dakar and its own Casamance province south of Gambian territory where freedom fighters undermine Senegal's own borders.

Since his most recent election success in September 2006, President Jammeh has continued to plough an individualist furrow through international relations. In December 2006 he made a three-day visit to Iran to meet with President Ahmadinejad and defended the country's right to develop nuclear weapons. In January 2007, the President announced that he had been given a mandate from the spirit world to cure illnesses, including asthma and HIV, through herbal potions and the laying on of hands. Long queues of expectant patients now form outside State House on the morning of Jammeh's 'surgeries', but scientists and doctors across Africa are appalled by this turn of events.

Bumsters – friend or foe?

With a lively patter and a 'never say die' attitude, 'bumsters' are a ubiquitous part of the holiday scene on The Gambia's tourist coast. They operate on the fringes of the tourist industry, hoping to take a slice of the cash generated here.

For many first-timers to The Gambia, the attentions of the bumsters are the one negative in an otherwise enjoyable holiday. But many of the people who return to The Gambia year after year feel that the bumsters are getting a raw deal. They have made friends with many and see them simply as genial guys trying to make a living.

A smiling beach bumster

Some bumsters hang around the tourist resorts hoping to pick up work as a guide, or tout for a restaurant or boat trip. Other young fit men hang around the beaches – women holidaying without men will certainly get plenty of attention – and for women of 'a certain age', The Gambia is known to be a source of very attentive holiday escorts.

Control and licensing

In the last few years the government has recognised that bumsters are one of the major causes of negative feedback about their country and a great deal has been done to clean up the business. A licensing system has been introduced to help visitors identify the professionals, and official 'Tourist Guides' can be found in or close to all the major hotels; you can hire them by the hour, the day or longer.

On the beaches, licensed fruit sellers and souvenir stalls have been installed in cute little tropical-style kiosks and they don't roam along the beach touting for business. Even the juice pressers have an association. The latest buzz words are professionalism and sustainability.

A bumster selling to tourists on Palm Beach, Kotu

How to deal with bumsters

These steps have made a big difference since 2000, but still, even with the licensing of some vendors, you are bound to be approached on the beach or on the tourist 'strips' as you sunbathe or head out to find something to eat. Often the guys will sidle up with a friendly hello and engage you on how your day is going – looking for an 'in' for their services. There's no need to feel afraid or intimidated, they are not aggressive, but you'll need to be firm if you want to be left alone. This may happen several times during the course of the day so it's easy to become short-tempered if you feel you can't get a moment to yourself, but here are a few tips to help you cope.

Be polite but be firm

- Don't say maybe if you mean no; bumsters remember.
- Keep smiling and wish them a good day.
- Tell them you hope they find some good business but you are not interested.
- Start as you mean to go on and stay true to your word. Bumsters will respect a 'no' proffered in a confident manner.

A final word

If you feel that a bumster has stepped over the line and is harassing rather than persuading, you can file a report with the tourist police (*see p147*). This special force has been set up specifically to help visitors with nuisance or crime.

Culture

The cultural norms in The Gambia are very different to those in Europe or North America. Exploring these differences is one of the most fascinating elements of a visit to the country. The people of 'The Smiling Coast' are happy to tell you about their lives and their communities where, beyond the coastal area, life has changed little for many generations.

The Gambian village

Families live in compounds made up of several huts surrounded by a fence for privacy and security. Very few compounds have fresh water, so in the country, villages are serviced by a community well and in towns by standpipes. Most compounds don't have electricity either, so families socialise around small *attaya* stoves in summer and around fires that are used to heat the cool winter evenings. Tasks are divided according to sex. The men are responsible for the rebuilding and re-thatching of the compound huts and for planting at the start of the rainy season. Men also spend lots of time sat on the *bantaba*, a large metal or bamboo seating area at the heart of the village, where the business of the day is discussed and much time is spent in jocular wordplay or in games of backgammon. Women are responsible for tending and harvesting crops, collecting water, cooking, childcare and all domestic chores.

TEA CEREMONY

Brewing Gambian tea or *attaya* is a time-honoured ritual that punctuates all social and ceremonial occasions and forms an important activity after dark when friends get together. To start the process, you'll need a small enamel teapot and a small square charcoal burner, easily bought at all Gambian markets.

Attaya is made using green gunpowder tea from China. Put one whole packet in the teapot with a small amount of water and sugar and let it boil on the burner. Pour the tea into a small glass tumbler, then pour it backwards and forwards into another tumbler until a foam develops. This foam should be equal to the volume of tea. Then sip the tea loudly through the foam. Each packet of tea is used to make three brews. The first and strongest is traditionally for the men. The second brew is weaker and has more sugar added, so it is said to be the woman's drink. The third is weakest and sweetest, for children and the elderly.

Religion

Over 90 per cent of the Gambian population is Muslim, with a minority of Christians – denominations range from Catholic to Anglican, Wesleyan to

A typical rural village

Seventh-Day Adventist. However, although monotheism is an important element in life, many Gambians also infuse their beliefs with a pagan animism (belief that supernatural powers influence life) symbolised by the use of spells and *jujus* (charms imbued with powers). The fortune-teller/herbalist/witchdoctor is a much-revered individual, especially in Jola society, and is consulted about all manner of things from the timing of travel to the auspiciousness of a business deal. Many Gambians wear a talisman next to the skin, to protect against evil spirits. The continued veneration of the crocodile, including visiting their freshwater pools, is a practice that predates the deities.

Body culture

Breasts are not considered sexual parts of the body in Western Africa and you may see women breast-feeding without embarrassment when you visit villages. The most erotic parts of a woman's body are considered to be the thighs, which is why women wear long dresses or skirts that flow over these areas rather than drawing attention to them.

Marriage

Polygamy is legal in The Gambia and it's not unusual for a man to have two or three wives living in the family compound. The husband has his own hut or bedroom and is visited by each wife in turn for two nights before taking a night's rest. Not surprisingly,

BANTABA

Bantaba is from where the English word banter, meaning 'a friendly exchange of teasing remarks', derives. The *Oxford English Dictionary* states that the word is '17th century: origin unknown' but the date certainly tallies with the arrival of the British in the region.

Gambian males set great store in the restorative effects of plants like African laburnum, which are touted as a natural form of Viagra.

Marriages are usually arranged by the parents of the couple, though not against the will of the couple themselves. Traditionally, negotiations take place between the male heads of household after an initial gift of kola nuts is received by the woman's parents, and the marriage contract also involves more presents of nuts, cash and/or other goods. The woman's family must provide her with all the things she'll need to set up home. Sometimes it is many months between the ceremony and the wife moving to the man's compound, as families raise sufficient funds for these dowries.

Circumcision

Circumcision in males is universal in The Gambia and over 80 per cent of females are also circumcised, usually between the ages of eight and twelve. Aside from the question of whether this is a necessary and ethical practice, circumcision has always marked the passage from childhood to adulthood in Gambian society and has been accompanied by long and grave initiation regimes.

To commence the process, boys traditionally depart the village to attend 'bush school', where an elder teaches them the rules and behaviours expected of them as adults, including sex education. At bush school the boys are protected by *kangkurang* (Mandinka) or *kumpo* (Jola) spirit guides who keep evil spirits at bay. They are then circumcised by the village blacksmith, and after a period of recuperation return to their compounds where their families throw a big party to celebrate their new status and welcome them back into the world. Circumcised boys sleep in a separate hut away from the women until they take a wife of their own. Today, bush school is much less popular, especially in the Kombos, and many elders point to this change as one of the reasons for the kinds of ills that seem to have befallen society, including crime, spousal abuse and rude behaviour.

TOUBAB

Toubab is the Wolof word meaning 'white man'. It is now used by people of all Gambian ethnic groups to describe light-skinned visitors of either sex, and you'll most often here it shouted by children as they wave excitedly at you from their village compounds.

Gambian women always wear long, flowing dresses

The tribes of The Gambia

Society in The Gambia is made up of a number of discrete ethnic groups who are found not only here but across a whole swathe of Western Africa. Many Gambians have family ties in neighbouring French-speaking Senegal, Mali and beyond.

Mandinka

By far the most widespread peoples of The Gambia, the Mandinka comprise over 40 per cent of the total population.

Mandinka is a hierarchical society ruled by age and social standing – there has also traditionally been a ruling noble clan. Their history is passed down through the *griots,* a clan of *kora*-playing storytellers.

Mandinka men wear a brimless cap, and a voluminous kaftan worn

Mandinka ritual performer

over loose trousers, while women wear tight-fitting 'bodiced' dresses with plunging backs, ruffled sleeves and slight bustles – inspired by the fashions of the European colonial women during the 18th and 19th centuries.

Jola

The Jola are thought by anthropologists to have been the earliest arrivals to the region. The most animist of the tribes – even though they are Muslim – there is still a deep belief in, and production of, *jujus*, spells and magical potions. The Jola traditionally lived in large villages of several thousand individuals but without a tribal chief or ruling clan.

One clan of the Jola are the Manjago, who traditionally undertake 'palm tapping'. The Manjago are Christian and/or animist and are also the only clan to keep pigs.

Jola men wear baggy trousers and shirts with waistcoats. The women's headdress has a corner which falls over the face.

Fula

Widespread across Western Africa, the Fula are the second-largest group in the country. Traditionally cattle

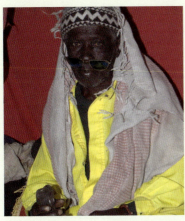
A traditional healer (witch doctor) from Tunjina

herders, they led a semi-nomadic existence and accumulated few possessions. One example of this is the main instrument, the *riti* – a type of flute that was easily transportable.

Fula women sport large amounts of gold jewellery and tattoos around the mouth or on the face. Men wear tunics of rough cotton and conical straw hats.

Wolof

A minority within the country's population, the Wolof are thought to have been descended originally from African royalty and reached The Gambia from Mauritania. They dominated trade and are now heavily involved in tourism. Traditional Wolof society was hierarchical with many castes. Today, social standing is measured more by wealth or education.

Wolof men wear long kaftans and the women look striking in their colourful, voluminous full-length dresses worn over a full-length skirt and high head ties.

Wolof men are renowned drummers.

Serahule

Rulers of the Kingdom of Ghana and the pre-eminent tradesmen of West Africa, the Serahule arrived in The Gambia in the 19th century as refugees, escaping war in their own country. Traders in gold and silver – the women wear large gold earrings decorated with red cord.

Serer

One of the oldest tribes in the Senegambia, the Serer are traditionally fishermen. Their heartland is in the Nuimi district around Barra on the north shore. According to oral history, they were enslaved by the Fula.

Aku

Descendants of freed slaves that returned to Africa in the 19th century, the Aku are often mixed race, the result of liaisons between slave women and colonial slave masters, with names such as Williams, Barry or Jones. They spoke Creole, not an African tribal language, and their English was often very good.

Festivals and events

Celebrations in The Gambia range from the all-singing, all-dancing national events such as Independence Day, to more intimate family occasions that commemorate important life stages.

NATIONAL EVENTS
Independence Day (18 February)
The main event is held in Banjul with military parades and marches centred on July 22 Square; however, all the main towns have some sort of official parade or event.

Kanilai Cultural Festival (every odd year, end May)
Inaugurated to coincide with the President's birthday on the 25th, this cultural festival celebrates all things Gambian with traditional songs and dances and is an opportunity to see authentic Gambian wrestling.

The International Roots Festival (every other year, one week during June)
The biggest event of the year, when The Gambia throws open its doors to its African American brethren and the African Diaspora travel over for a spiritual and very emotional homecoming. Hundreds arrive in Juffereh to re-enact the final moments of Kunte Kinte and to meet with the family. They are welcomed by hundreds of villagers from *griots* and elders to singing schoolchildren. But beyond the historical north-shore locations, the whole of The Gambia erupts into life with cultural concerts and tribal dancing, culinary festivals and special markets – the whole country seems to get involved.

Liberation Day (22 June)
To commemorate the coup that ousted the previous regime in 1994, President Jammeh gives a rousing speech and there are nationwide celebrations.

RELIGIOUS FESTIVALS
Maolud Nabi
The Prophet Mohammed's birthday is spent in reflection with readings from the Koran and messages from the Imam.

Koriteh
This feast marks the end of Ramadan, the yearly period of fasting. Muslims

will start the day with prayers and then there is a huge celebratory meal when family and friends dress up and get together. Koriteh is a time when family members working away will try to get home, which puts tremendous strain on bush taxi systems throughout the country.

Tobaski (also Tabaski)

The Feast of the Sacrifice coincides with The Hajj pilgrimage to Mecca and takes place two months and ten days after the end of Ramadan. The head of the family sacrifices a goat, as Ismail did, and the family sit down to give thanks. This is another festival where family members working away from home will return, even if only for the day.

SOCIAL AND FAMILY FESTIVALS
Naming Day Ceremony

The Naming Day marks the official welcome of a new baby into society and it's an important social occasion for the individual and for the family. One week after the birth the elders of the village gather at the family compound. A tribal elder cuts a lock of the baby's hair and an animal is sacrificed as the name is said. In Mandinka families a *griot* or *jeli* sings traditional songs during the ceremony. The family and friends then sit down to a meal and the celebrations go on into the night with traditional drumming, singing and dancing.

Circumcision rite of passage

After girls and boys have been circumcised (*see p20*) and spent time in bush school, they return home to their families as adults. In their absence, the family will have prepared new clothes and shoes and there's a huge family feast with *masquerede* dancing at which costumed, masked or stilted guides such as the *kangkurang* or *kumpo* will appear to keep away evil spirits.

Many events are celebrated with music and dancing

Highlights

Page	
32	Banjul
42	Serrekunda & the tourist coast
64	The north shore
80	Janjangbureh (Georgetown) & the mid-river region

N

SENEGAL

GUINEA-BISSAU

THE GAMBIA

SENEGAL

Fatoto

Vélingara

Basse

Koussanar

Karantaba

Maka

River Gambia

Bansang

Koungheul

Wassu Stones

Kuntaur

Janjangbureh

River Gambia National Park

Kolda

Kau-ur

Farafenni

Soma

Kaolack

Soungrougrou

Sédhiou

Casamance

Bao Bolong Wetland Reserve

Kiang West National Park

Kerewan

River Gambia

THE GAMBIA

Toubacouta

Ziguinchor

Bignona

Barra

BANJUL

Juffereh

James Island

Albreda

Makasutu Cultural Forest

Salcum Delta National Park

Bakua

Abuko Nature Reserve

Banjul International

Brikama

❶ ❷ ❸ ❹ ❺ ❻ ❼ ❽ ❾

1 **Albert Market, Banjul** Shopping in Albert Market in Banjul, the capital's lively open-air bazaar offers a rich slice of West African daily life.

2 **Abuko Nature Reserve** Exploring Abuko Nature Reserve, the most accessible of The Gambia's many protected natural areas.

3 **Makasutu Cultural Forest** Touching the trees in the Makasutu Cultural Forest; this sacred place is now an award winning eco-attraction.

4 **Stepping onto James Island** Many thousands of Africans left this small island for a life of slavery in the 'New World'.

5 **Kinte clan at Juffureh** Shaking the hand of the head of the Kinte clan at Juffureh, descendants of Kunte Kinte, the first of *Roots* author Alex Haley's relatives to land on American soil to be sold into slavery.

6 **Wassu Stones** Gazing at the Wassu Stones, the most ancient man-made structures in the country and the only evidence of a long-lost society.

7 **Kiang West National Park** Tramping through the forest of Kiang West National Park, the most diverse ecosystem in The Gambia, protecting more flora and fauna than any other in the country.

8 **Bao Bolong Wetland Reserve** Discovering the inlets of Bao Bolong Wetland Reserve, a world-renowned wetland area and a haven for wading birds.

9 **River Gambia cruises** Cruising on the River Gambia, to enjoy the tempo of life on the water that is the lifeblood of the country.

Village life Visiting a Gambian village, to learn about life in the rural heartland.

A musician playing *kora* music at Makasutu Cultural Forest

Suggested itineraries

Despite the fact that The Gambia is a small country, travelling times should never be underestimated and will play a large part in deciding where you visit during your trip, whatever the amount of time you have. With many of the country's best attractions being both natural and unpredictable (animals and birds don't appear on cue), factoring in time and flexibility is an absolute must. This is one destination where you can't expect travel plans to go 100 per cent smoothly, especially if you want to leave the coast and explore inland.

A long weekend or midweek break

If you intend to spend only a short time in the country – a long weekend of four or so days – you'll be better off staying in the western coastal areas: the district known as Kombo or the Kombos. You are sure to want to enjoy the beach for at least part of your trip and you should programme in a day or a couple of afternoons of doing absolutely nothing but soaking in the sun.

Spend a morning exploring the capital; shopping in Albert Market introduces you to West African urban life. Soak in the atmosphere of the bustling alleyways and snack on peanuts or cashew nuts (grown in the countryside here) as you browse.

It's also important to spend some time on the river, so book a cruise in a traditional wooden pirogue. Early birds can catch the morning chorus (but it does mean getting to the boat by 6.45am), or take a mid-afternoon trip. Either way you'll spend three or four hours among the mangroves with only birdsong and the tapping of oyster fisherwomen's machetes breaking the silence.

Abuko Nature Reserve is the closest protected tract of land to the coastal strip, so it's easy to take a taxi to explore and spend as much time as you like watching the birds, monkeys, crocodiles and deer. Makasutu Cultural Forest offers similar forestscapes but has several differences to Abuko, not least of which is the delicious buffet lunch that's served in the restaurant (pre-book or arrive as part of a group) and the wooden deck where you can have a cooling drink and watch the activity on Mandina Bolong. Makasutu offers a chance to tour the *bolongs* on dugout canoes, and the forest has a large troop of baboons who treat the man-made structures with disdain – great fun if you are lucky enough to be there when they come through. This sacred place is now an award-winning cultural eco-attraction.

You should also take time to explore the traditional lifestyles of Gambians, and the easiest way to do this is to visit a village compound. It's a humbling experience to discover how simply the vast majority of the population live, and to learn about daily life in Africa.

Don't forget to get out of the hotel in the evening to enjoy the bars and restaurants of the Senegambia strip or the western end of Kairaba Avenue. The folkloric performance on Saturday evenings at Makasutu is also a must.

The major ground tour operators along the coast organise day tours incorporating several activities listed above on the same itinerary with transport and lunch included. If you don't want the trouble of organising your time and transport yourself, this is a great way to discover the attractions of the Kombos.

A week

A few more days means you can factor in time to leave the Kombos and travel

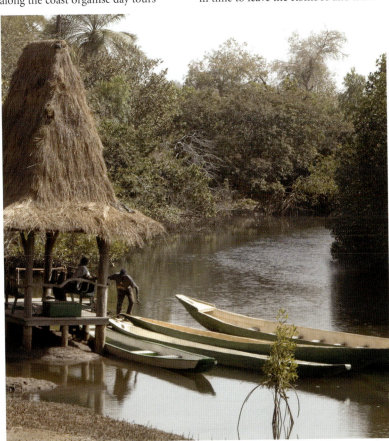

Explore the *bolongs* of Makasutu in a canoe

A hyena at Abuko Nature Reserve

up-country (east towards central Africa). The most obvious extra activity is to follow the *Roots* trail and immerse yourself in the story of slavery in The Gambia. You can meet the African descendants of author Alex Haley at their family compound at Juffureh and take a trip to James Island, the British headquarters from where hundreds of thousands of Africans were exported against their will to the Caribbean and the Americas.

A different excursion allows you to visit Kanilai, birthplace of President Jammeh, to enjoy the Game Park and have lunch at Sindola Lodge.

Two weeks

Spending two weeks in The Gambia gives you enough time to visit much of the mid-river region in addition to enjoying the attractions on the coast. A four-night itinerary allows you to spend time at all of The Gambia's up-country national parks and to visit the standing stone circles at Wassu.

On day one, once across the river, follow the North Shore road to spend some time at Bao Bolong National Park before building speed to reach your lodge at Janjangbureh (Georgetown) before nightfall. The next day, explore the town and retrace your steps to the North Shore for the 15-minute journey to Wassu to visit these most ancient structures. Give day three over to a boat trip along the river to take in the River Gambia National Park and catch sight of chimps at the rehabilitation project and hippos wallowing in the shallows, then return to Janjangbureh for the night. On day four prepare for the 'route from hell' as you tackle the southern arterial road heading back for the coast. Set off early to reach Tendaba by lunchtime, then take a boat trip or trek into Kiang West National Park, home to leopards and caracals, then overnight at Tendaba Camp. If you powered on past Bao Bolong on day one you can get to the park by boat from Tendaba, so factor in an extra day here. Finally, on day five (or day six), return to the coast for a well-earned rest.

Longer?

The ultimate vessel for really getting under the skin of The Gambia must be a wooden pirogue. This vessel allows you to travel with the rhythm of the river, hopping on and off exactly where you want to and exploring the countryside. Take a bicycle and visit rural villages, as nothing is very far from the water and you can allow the local pace of life to pull you in. If you do want to make this a once-in-a-lifetime trip and include all the attractions above, you'll need to give yourself 10–14 days.

Suggested itineraries

Local women in Janjangbureh

Banjul

When the British wanted to defend the mouth of the Gambia River against the French and Portuguese just after the abolition of slavery within the empire, they built a fortress on either bank. St Mary's Island, the most northerly point of dry land on the south bank, had its advantages, being protected by an impenetrable maze of mangrove bolongs on its western flank – so Bathurst was born in 1816. Over time the settlement blossomed into the capital, which was renamed Banjul in 1973.

Not without its charms, Banjul has suffered a great reversal of fortune in the modern age, hemmed in by a veritable swathe of mangrove, known as the Tanbi Wetlands, that proved such an asset 150 years before. It couldn't contain the burgeoning population and most made the decision to move to less crowded accommodation around Serrekunda to the south. Today its permanent population is less than 40,000.

During daylight hours Banjul seethes with activity. Hundreds of civil servants head to desk jobs in government departments, nurses to shifts at the country's teaching hospital, the Royal Victoria, and secondary-school pupils to lessons at Gambia Senior Secondary School. Almost every fisherman, shopkeeper, market trader and shopper lives outside the city and travels in and out daily along the one arterial road cutting through the wetland, packed into old, noisy bush taxis and buses. Add to this the foot and heavy goods traffic from ferries linking Banjul to Barra on the north coast (one of only three places where commercial traffic can cross the river, and a major conduit for traffic from northern Senegal and southern Senegal) and you have organised chaos. You think that your commute is difficult; just wait until you witness this.

Sandy swathes bound the city on its northern and western flanks from where a colourful fishing fleet heads out to sea. From here it's possible to take in the immense size of the river just before it disgorges into the sea. Across the aching mouth one can just make out the town of Barra on the north bank.

Albert Market

Aside from its role as a capital, Banjul has one *raison d'être*: trade. The streets are lined with shops, and impromptu stalls pop up on every street corner selling everything from towels to fake watches. Vendors even stroll the streets selling goods out of suitcases; it's the

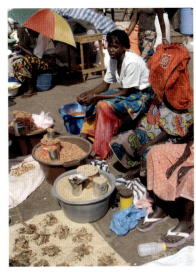

Albert Market

deal that counts. The best place to really soak in this mercantile atmosphere is at Albert Market, a huge labyrinth of permanent stalls supplemented by thousands of smallholders selling a few freshly picked fruits or vegetables beautifully displayed on a piece of clean cloth set out on the ground. Vendors and customers cram together and stevedores steer through the melee, barrows piled high with produce. Fruit and vegetables, fish and meat, each has its own section; then there are fabrics, clothes, toiletries and numerous curious objects and produce that you'll just need to guess at, like the thin sticks of wood that Gambians use to rub their teeth to keep them clean, or grotesque-looking roots to be boiled in water and said to be as powerful as Viagra. Albert Market has a large craft and souvenir

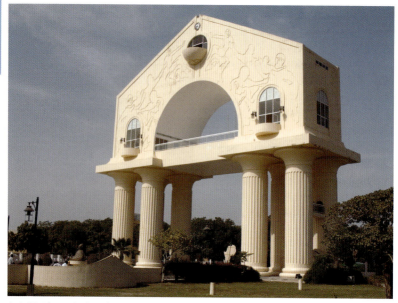

Arch 22 July marks the military coup of 1994

section and the stallholders are a jovial crowd. Most of the merchandise is mass-produced – colourful bangles and necklaces or wooden carvings of animals – though there are a couple of stalls selling good-quality drums and other African instruments. If you find something you like, you'll need to bargain hard to get a good price.
Off Russell Street. Open: daily 8am–7pm.

Arch 22 July

Banjul's most visible edifice was commissioned by President Jammeh to commemorate the military coup that brought him to power and liberated The Gambia on 22 July 1994. The arch was designed to stand as a monument to the founding of a new, forward-looking regime; however, with an estimated price tag of just over one million US dollars, some might argue that the money would have been better spent elsewhere.

Designed by Pierre Goudiaby, a Senegalese architect and favourite of Jammeh, the arch spans the southern end of Independence Drive and marks the entrance to the city from the main highway. Eight mammoth Doric columns, large enough to house lifts and spiral staircases, support the main structure. Sadly, the lifts are no longer working because settlement into the soft substrate has caused the shafts to change shape.

Climb the stairs to the intermediate level where the terrace offers excellent views across the Banjul skyline. From here the single-storey, corrugated-roofed family homes form a dense patchwork interspersed with low-rise office buildings. You get a real feel for how small the city is that's difficult to grasp when you are trying to negotiate the crowded streets.

Unfortunately, because traffic isn't allowed to pass beneath it (except for the cars of the President and high government officials), the arch causes long queues at adjacent road intersections. On the north side are the gardens decorated with statues of traditional musicians by Goudiaby's brother that were originally gilded but that have completely lost their glossy veneer.

Independence Drive. Open: daily 8am–4pm. Admission charge.

Denton Bridge

The only crossing point linking Banjul with the rest of southern Gambia, Denton Bridge is busy with traffic at all times of the day. There's little to hold people here, but the jetties on the inland side of the bridge are the home bases for most of the boats that tour the *bolongs* – so most people who book a boat trip will find themselves here at one time or another – be it 'Birds and Breakfast' at 5.30am or 'Sunset Cruise' at 5.30pm. This makes Denton Bridge the gateway to a whole different Gambia; one of tidal mangroves, sandbanks, herons and ospreys, and the

Boats at Denton Bridge

relative silence of the natural world. *On the western approach 5km (3 miles) from Banjul.*

King Fahad Mosque

The Gambia's largest mosque was built with funds gifted by the King of Saudi Arabia, after whom it is named, and it opened in 1988. It's a total contrast to the many intimate neighbourhood and village mosques where a hundred or so people might gather on Friday lunchtime for the main weekly prayer meeting. At King Fahad Mosque there's a large internal courtyard and an immense sandy outer courtyard with a capacity of thousands, and one can imagine the impression these masses of people praying together would have on a first-time visitor or a young child.

Still, most of the time the mosque is a very quiet place. The architectural form is elegant, with beige stucco emphasising the clean lines. However, its main impact is in its size; the twin minarets punctuate the skyline, even visible as you arrive by air, and the overall footprint is the largest in the city.
Box Bar Road. Open: dawn–dusk except during prayer times. Free admission.

National Museum

Housed in the old Bathurst Club building, where colonial stalwarts would meet for a G&T and listen to cricket on the radio, the country's principal national collection could be so interesting. A range of artefacts chronicling the history of Senegambia, both geologically and anthropologically, with a little imagination the displays could offer much but in reality they interest few, like the dry old history textbooks some of us had to learn from at school. But I urge you to look further. It's a bit like shopping at a car boot sale; there are treasures to be found especially for anyone with an interest in the development of Africa as a continent, and particularly the ground-floor displays charting the development of The Gambia pre- and post-Independence. There's an interesting display charting the development of early societies in the region and background information about the arrival of Islam.

The collection ranges from the usual (old maps of the country and historical documents) to the bizarre, such as the dress worn by Miss Gambia when she won the beauty contest in 1984.
Independence Drive. Open: Mon–Thur 8am–4pm, Fri–Sat 8am–1pm. Admission charge.

St Mary's Cathedral

This unassuming painted-brick church, completed in the 1930s, is the centre for Anglican worship in The Gambia. Kept neat and tidy by the small Protestant community, it sees far fewer worshippers than it did during colonial rule.

The decorative highlight of the simple interior is an ornate tapestry depicting scenes from the Bible transposed into the African landscape.

To the right of the cathedral as you look towards the façade is July 22 Square, a parade ground renamed after the military coup. Today it's the venue for lavish Independence Day ceremonies and other celebrations. President Jammeh takes place of honour along with other dignitaries in the grandstand on the western flank.

Close by on Leman Street is Our Lady of the Assumption Cathedral, completed in 1916 and the leading Catholic place of worship.
Independence Drive. Open: Mon–Sat 8am–7pm, Sun noon–7pm.
Free admission.

State House

The seat of the President sits on the northernmost point of St Mary's Island. In the grounds are the remains of Six-Gun Battery, the original cannon delivered to Bathurst when the city was founded. Unfortunately, even these were not powerful enough to fire missiles across the full width of the river, and enemy shipping merely paralleled the north shore to avoid being hit. It was for this reason that Fort Bullen (*see p68*) was added on the north shore in the late 1820s.
Independence Drive. Not open to the public.

St Mary's Cathedral is a modest building

Walk: Downtown Banjul

Banjul is a compact capital brimming with life. A stroll around introduces you to the energy of African life.

Allow 4 hours.

Distance: 5km (3 miles) including return to car.

See p32 for a map of the route.

Park your car on the verge of the street leading left from Arch 22 (signposted Atlantic Hotel) and you'll be able to return to it later. Cross the street and you'll enter the small park at the top of Independence Drive.

1 Arch 22 July

Arch 22 July celebrates the military coup that brought the current president, Jammeh, to power in 1994. It dominates the cityscape rather like the bouffant hairstyle on the head of a slender woman. However, there are views across the whole city from the viewing platform on the intermediate level.
From the base of the arch, face down Independence Drive but don't walk down there just yet. Turn right down Wallace Cole Road for 300m (330yds) and you'll find King Fahad Mosque on the left.

2 King Fahad Mosque

King Fahad Mosque was built by money donated by the King of Saudi Arabia. It's the largest in The Gambia.

You can enter if it's not prayer time, but remember to remove your shoes and dress modestly.
Return to the arch and begin walking down Independence Drive. With government offices at the western end, it's free from all but official traffic, but when it becomes Nancy Pierre Road just after the Royal Victoria Teaching Hospital, the route becomes busier. Seven hundred metres (770yds) from Arch 22 July, you find the National Museum on the left.

3 National Museum

The Gambia's major anthropological and folkloric collection isn't the most high tech around but has some interesting artefacts to enjoy.
From the museum, continue walking east (away from the arch). After another 150m (160yds), the cream-painted St Mary's Cathedral sits at the roadside.

4 St Mary's Cathedral

The cathedral is a 1930s brick-built structure with a simple, serene interior.

The pews are made out of fine mahogany, a wood now in short supply. *Continue your journey east once again. After the cathedral you'll pass July 22 Square and venue for The Gambia's ebullient Independence Day parades. Just after the square, Nancy Pierre Road meets a main intersection.*

5 Monument to the Unknown Soldier

Traffic wheels around a small roundabout on which stands an almost forgotten but poignant monument to the Unknown Soldier.
Turn left at the intersection, keeping July 22 Square on your left. After 150m (160yds), cross the street and take a right down Liberation Avenue (also signposted Russell Street). The entrances to Albert Market are just on your left.

6 Albert Market

Albert Market is the best location to grasp the daily essence of life in modern The Gambia. Take in the smells; the sights; the faces – and, of course, do a little shopping. Don't forget to haggle!
Leave the craft market section of Albert Market at the northwestern end and cross the grubby street to reach the beach. Turn right and after 200m (220yds) you'll find the fishing fleet pulled up on the sand.

7 Fish Market

The fish market here is very busy early morning and in the evening. Between times you'll find the ladies cleaning and preparing, and the men tending the nets.
After a refreshing drink at Omar's Beach Bar, the quickest way back to the car is to retrace your steps.

The National Museum has some fascinating exhibits

Boat tour from Denton Bridge

All vehicular traffic arriving or departing from Banjul has to cross Denton Bridge, which spans a large bolong *that cuts through the Tanbi wetlands. These wetlands offer hundreds of hectares of tidal mangrove replete with bird life that seems a world away from the bustle of the capital or the nearby tourist coast. Most of the tour boat trips offered by tour operators depart from Denton Bridge, but don't expect a cruise-port-type welcome centre. The Denton Bridge facility is simply a couple of wooden jetties with one unpretentious café.*

Allow 4 hours.

Distance: 20km (12 miles).

Once you've made yourself comfortable, the boat will depart, heading south along the Oyster Creek.

1 Oyster Creek

The oyster harvesters work here, in the mangrove roots where the oysters develop, cutting them free with machetes. The women may spend many hours waist-deep in the water before returning to the shore to smoke their catch.
After 1km (½ mile), the boat takes a left turn down a meandering tributary called Turnbull Bolong.

2 Turnbull Bolong

The north bank of the *bolong* is actually the southern boundary of Banjul Island and the impenetrable morass of mangrove is one of the reasons why the city could not expand beyond its constrictive boundaries. Turnbull Bolong offers close-quarter views of the mangrove banks. Here's the place to spot Western Reef herons and whimbrels in the shallows while Goliath herons and ospreys fly overhead.

After approximately 2km (1 mile) Turnbull Bolong opens out into Chitabong Bolong.

3 Chitabong Bolong

The vista that greets your eyes here would seem like a seascape, but what you are actually looking at is the vast expanse of the River Gambia. It's over 20km (12 miles) directly across to the north shore from here, and often the long-distance view is shrouded in haze. To the left you'll see the southern tip of Banjul city, with the ferry dock at Barra the most obvious landmark.

The boat turns right here, away from the capital and towards Chitabong, Duranka and the Lamin islands.

4 Iron Hulled Ships

The hulls of several old iron ships can be seen here. Left rotting in the shallows, they have become a favourite roost for pink-backed pelicans.

Beyond the islands, after 2.5km (1½ miles), the channel narrows and the boat makes its way into Lamin Bolong.

5 Lamin Lodge

At the head of Lamin Bolong sits Lamin Lodge, for many years a popular stop en route for a swim or a drink. A true jungle shack made entirely of local wood, the lodge is currently closed but it still makes an excellent photo opportunity. Look out for families of monkeys playing on the rafters.

From Lamin Lodge the boat turns for home. Returning to the entrance of Lamin Bolong, it turns left into Duranka Bolong.

6 Duranka Bolong

The leisurely journey back allows plenty more time for bird-spotting. Look out for chattering pied kingfishers, sacred ibis and perhaps a spoonbill or two.

Eventually, after 10km (6 miles), Duranka Bolong meets the intersection with Oyster Bolong, and Denton Bridge will come into view ahead through the collection of masts. Your craft will draw quietly to the jetty, bringing your trip to an end.

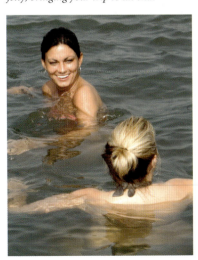

Cool off in the water at Denton Bridge

Serrekunda and the tourist coast

The coast south of the River Gambia is the country's tourist heartland, where all its large resorts sit within metres of long, fine-sand beaches bedecked by swaying palms. It's the stuff that holiday dreams are made of and over 90 per cent of The Gambia's visitors will book accommodation here, along a short stretch from Cape Point in the north, down through Kotu to Kololi in the south.

Vervet monkeys in Abuko Nature Reserve

Handfuls of inexpensive restaurants, beach bars and nightclubs make this a user-friendly tourist coast, but always a certain something reminds you that you're in Africa, be it the monkeys that flit across the roads or the booming of the drums – a sound that seems to beat the air, setting up a kind of Gambian heartbeat wherever you go.

But the Kombos, as the region is also known, offers much more than simple rest and relaxation. There are numerous attractions set among the verdant mangrove-swathed coastline or the inland forests. You could fill a week with things to do, and ecotourism is beginning to make an impact with several small-scale sustainable projects created by the communities themselves.

Abuko Nature Reserve

The most accessible of The Gambia's protected areas, Abuko is an easy taxi ride from the resorts and offers a real opportunity to view some of the country's finest wildlife at close quarters. If you don't intend to visit any of the other national parks, then you should spend a couple of hours here, soaking in the real feel of wild Africa.

The reserve was created by conservation pioneer Eddie Brewer in the 1960s when he fenced a tract of savannah, tropical forest and gallery forest (woodland lining a stream or river) flanking the Lamin Bolong to protect the native trees and wildlife. Here you'll find one of very few year-round waterholes (called Bamboo Pool)

A makeshift bridge in the nature reserve

in the region, which supports many large tree species and attracts a whole range of animals, reptiles and birds – over 300 species have been spotted here. Abuko is one of the favoured rest stops for seasonal species who head into Europe in the summer months, and the park caters specifically to the needs of birdwatchers with several well-camouflaged hides. A single footpath snakes through the dense forest where you'll often find vervet monkeys scurrying along or foraging for food in the undergrowth. More secretive are the bushbuck deer, monitor lizards and the crocodiles, which steer clear of human contact if at all possible.

The Darwin Field Station, close to Bamboo Pool, is an education centre for students of biodiversity who come here to study the animals. Lay visitors will find a wealth of information about the species that live here, with useful photographs and details about diet, habitat and habits. The balcony on the upper floor has great views across the waterhole where, whatever time of the day, there is something fascinating to watch, be it the herons fishing in the shallows or snakes taking a welcome drink.

At the furthest reach of the footpath is a rather out-of-place Animal Orphanage, a wildlife rehabilitation facility set up in 1997 where baboons and other monkeys rescued from Gambian homes are supposedly being reprogrammed to return to the wild. You'll also find a permanent population of well-fed hyenas lounging around, little troubled by the human visitors who stare at them through the fence.

For the best possible chance of seeing plenty of wildlife, arrive at Abuko early in the morning (before 10am) or late in the afternoon, because in the heat of the day the animals are much less active. For those more particularly interested in spotting wildlife, you can arrange visits outside normal park hours when you may be rewarded by views of rare and shy native fauna.

On the main road north of Abuko village. Open: daily 8am–6pm. Admission charge.

Bakau

Like Serrekunda, Bakau has grown quickly in the last 20 years into a maze of narrow streets surrounding the nucleus of the old town. Most visitors make for the Katchikally Crocodile Tank (*see p49*) just to the south of town, but the real delight of a visit is its contrast with the tourist coastal strip just a couple of kilometres to the west. If you can rise above the constant '*toubab*-ing' from endless herds of cheeky kids, it's a fascinating introduction to everyday urban African life. Try the local market, which isn't as large as that at Serrekunda but offers a similar kind of atmosphere. The *bengdula* (craft market) is also much more user-friendly, as all the stalls face the street, rather than being arranged on an enclosed interior courtyard.

Craft market at Atlantic Road. Open: daily 9am–6pm.

The craft market in Bakau

Brikama

A centre of handicrafts, Brikama is famed for its woodcarvers. The output from small artisan-owned workshops in the town supplies most of the beach and street vendors on the Kololi coast, and many of the craft stalls in the markets. It's not surprising that when you visit the craft market here you can buy a full range of the wooden items found all across the country – from giraffes to tribal masks – but you'll be able to chat to the people who carved them, many of whom have a latent talent passed down through generations of their families. Much of what you find 'front of shop' is the same as elsewhere along the coast, but if you want to avoid the kitsch, it's possible – the workshops lie just behind the area of the market stalls and the smell of fresh sawdust is a delicate accompaniment to your tour.

Get into discussion with an artisan and get them to carve you a bespoke piece; they'll relish and rise to the challenge. Just remember to agree a price first!

Wooden drums from Brikama

Most visitors to Fajara come for the golf

Brikama is also known through the Senegambia region for its musicians. Just as with woodcarving, many families have passed their musical talent through the generations and almost all current Gambian musical luminaries hail from the town (though they usually have to leave the country to build their careers).

Craft market on the main street. Open: daily 8am–7pm.

Fajara

The small coastal village squeezed between Bakua and Kotu owes much to the period of British colonial rule, with architecture that speaks of days gone by. Though it's set among the tourist resorts, it still feels a world apart and many visitors race through in taxis heading for other places.

Golf is the main reason to visit Fajara. The Fajara Country Club maintains the Fajara Golf Club immaculately even though the gardeners work to a different rulebook to the greens keepers back home. There's a range of other sports to enjoy too.

The tiny War Cemetery in the village is a poignant memorial to those who lost their lives during the Second World War when Banjul was an important staging post for both shipping and air services. Over 300 people lie buried here and there is a memorial to over 30 Gambians who died on other battlefields during the conflict.

Fajara Country Club. Atlantic Road. Tel: 449 5456. Greens open: daily. War Cemetery. Kairaba Avenue. Open access.

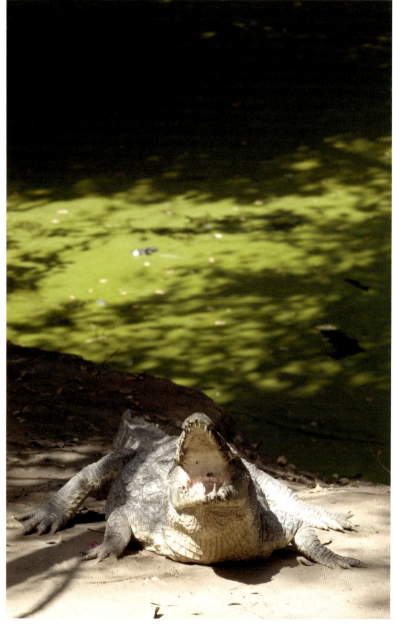

The Nile crocodile generally grows to around 4m (13ft) in The Gambia

Katchikally Crocodile Tank

The crocodile is a sacred animal to Gambians, revered for its great physical strength and for its mystical powers. The waterholes frequented by these crocodiles have become important in the country's animist rituals and even today great care and attention are lavished on the beasts, even more so since the natural habitat of the crocodiles is fast disappearing and they are becoming fewer in number.

Although it's not the only one in the region, the pool at Katchikally (also spelled Katchikali) is the most visited by tourists, with groups arriving regularly throughout the day. It might be easy to view this simply as another attraction, but your guide will be happy to go into greater detail about Gambian beliefs and rituals.

Katchikally has been made famous in modern times as the home of Charlie, the camera-hogging crocodile, who just loves to have his photograph taken with visitors. Streams of people step up to shake paws with Charlie or to stroke his back. He seems unconcerned at the fuss. The guides assure you that Charlie has never attempted to attack a human, though I wonder what the response of your travel insurance company would be if you ever had to make a claim!

Charlie is the photogenic crocodile, but he shares the pool with over 100 others ranging in size from 50cm (20in) babies to 3m (10ft) giants. They float on the water surface among the bright-green pondweed or bask in the sunshine on the banks. A few egrets also call the pond home, raising their chicks just a metre or so above a snout full of teeth, safe in the knowledge that few predators would dare to venture very close and risk being eaten by the giant reptiles.

Close to the entrance, the guardian family have created a small but very interesting folklore display with masks and musical instruments important to the local peoples and information about the native plants and their uses. *Off Salt Matty Road, Bakua. Open: daily dawn–dusk. Donation expected.*

THE SACRED POOLS

The crocodile is a powerful symbol in many West African cultures including all the peoples of The Gambia. A Mandinka legend states that a crocodile inhabits the Moon, while others view the creature as a link between the earthly life and the departed in the spirit world. Most prevalently, crocodiles are associated with fertility – the literal bringers of life, or the bestowers of good fortune and wealth.

Even today, infertile women come to bathe in the waters of the pool in a ritual designed to produce a pregnancy, and businessmen too, who want success in a new deal; even politicians have been known to visit at election time. However, few endanger themselves by bathing in the actual pool; there are shower cubicles carrying water pumped from the sacred source, and it's possible to take sacred water away to continue the rituals at home.

The pools are looked after by a guardian family, a responsibility passed down through the generations. Though they are not allowed to profit from their role for fear of upsetting the spirits, donations are gratefully accepted.

The life cycle of the crocodile

The Nile crocodile (*Crocodylus niloticus*) is top predator in waters of The Gambia. These flesh-eating reptiles are supremely adapted to their environment, having changed little since they evolved over 65 million years ago.

Environment

Nile crocodiles are at home in rivers and estuaries. Their noses and eyes sit at the very top of the head, allowing them to watch the banks while much of their body is submerged. For swimming and diving they have ears that close when submerged, clear third eyelids that cover the pupils allowing the animals to see underwater, and a muscular tail, webbed toes and short powerful limbs for speed.

Crocodiles spend many hours basking in the sun on sandy banks and tidal flats. This increases the body temperature and improves digestion. When adult, crocodiles can reduce their metabolic rate and heart beat, often remaining inactive for much of the day.

Diet

Young crocs feed on insects, frogs and small fish. For adult crocodiles, larger fish make up the bulk of their diet, though they do take warthog, bushbuck and other deer, waiting motionless in the water and making high-speed surprise attacks when the animals come to drink. Despite their impressive teeth, they cannot chew; those gnashers are for grabbing and holding. They simply swallow whole chunks of food, which are processed in the stomach. It was assumed that crocodiles required a lot of food, but research has shown that they have a very slow metabolism and a large meal can satisfy one for weeks. However, they can eat up to half their immense body weight at one sitting.

Reproduction

A large male will fight rivals to gain control of a stretch of river and will have a harem of females. Mating takes place in November and December and there is a three-month incubation period. Nests comprising large mounds of vegetable matter are built above high tide mark on the river banks. The female lays around 50 eggs and covers them so that the temperature remains constant.

The exact temperature decides the sex of the whole batch of eggs – if the temperature falls below 31.7°C (89°F) or rises above 34.5°C (94°F),

You can get quite close to these creatures, but be careful!

then the eggs will develop female young. Between these temperatures they will develop into males.

The mother protects the nest with great vigour. When the young start to hatch they call to her, stimulating her to dig them out and take them to the water. She stays with her hatchlings for the first few weeks. The eggs and young hatchlings suffer most attrition in the whole crocodile life cycle. Eggs are taken by predators, and young hatchlings (about 25cm/10in in length) make a perfect meal for large river fish, plus numerous bird species. Less than 5 per cent of eggs hatch and reach maturity.

Growth and lifespan
Young crocs grow at about 30cm (12in) per year. Sexual maturity happens in both sexes at about ten years of age. Adults found in The Gambia are not particularly large, usually under 4m (13ft), but examples across the continent have reached 6m (20ft) in length. The lifespan of the creatures has not been well documented; however, it's thought that they can live up to 100 years.

Kololi

The Gambia's most concentrated tourist development lies on the coast west of Kololi village and can be most neatly explained as development along the road leading to the coast from the main road (Bertil Harding Highway) at the Palma Rima Resort, and a parallel development along the road leading from the main road to the Senegambia Hotel, known affectionately by everyone as the 'Senegambia strip'.

The 'strip' is little more than 300m (330yds) in length but it's a great place for a beer and some passable food at one of 20 or so eateries. There's also an ATM here, though you might need to prompt the bank staff to fill it up with cash before you can use it. It's possible to walk between the two areas, but taxis are cheap, plentiful and more sensible after dark when there is no street lighting.

Kotu

Set around the outlet of the Kotu Stream, Kotu resort is little more than a handful of hotels, the best of which is the Kombo Beach, and restaurants backed up by a small craft market. However, it has arguably the best stretch of sand on the tourist coast and it's less high-paced than the 'Senegambia strip' in Kololi (*see above*). There is some excellent birdwatching on the doorstep around the river's edge. Where the main road crosses the river there's a hut where you can hire a government-approved guide, but unofficial 'bumster' guides appear from behind every bush. An impressive pair of binoculars doesn't necessarily make a good guide; ask to see an identity card!

Makasutu Cultural Forest

One of The Gambia's first forays into ecotourism and now receiving international acclaim, Makasutu is a unique project that couldn't have come to fruition without the efforts and enthusiasm of two Englishmen, James English and Laurence Williams. The two bought a small tract of gallery forest beside Mandina Bolong in 1992 and by 1999 owned 4sq km (1$\frac{1}{2}$sq miles). Initially they simply wanted to create a small travellers' motel. Today there's an award-winning lodge, a welcome centre, a nature trail and boat trips on the *bolong* – perfect for

A baboon in Makasutu Cultural Forest

Kotu beach is perfect for sun-worshipping

birdwatchers – and the most comprehensive information about the bird and animal species to be found anywhere in the country. The native wildlife has been left undisturbed to the extent that the troop of baboons that inhabit the forest may take it upon themselves to join you for lunch, wreaking havoc by raiding the rubbish bins and stealing bananas from plates, all to the great delight of the guests.

There's a much more serious side to Makasutu, however. The forest is invaluable as a habitat of ancient virgin forest with a rich biodiversity. English and Williams wanted to preserve and document this yet also make it a valuable resource for the community. To this end they employ dozens of local people as guides, restaurant staff and cooks; they have also worked tirelessly

to promote the Makasutu Wildlife Trust which, among other aims, encourages local education in biodiversity for Gambian schools. The trust is fostering links with international organisations including The Eden Project in the UK.

A tour of the forest brings you into contact with many valuable plants used by generations of Gambians for house construction, boatbuilding or natural medicines. You can visit a genuine traditional herbalist and fortune-teller, a much-revered member of traditional Gambian society, who will be able to tell you what your future has in store.

The Makasutu evening spectacular is a magical experience, with tribal dancers landing from a dugout canoe by the light of the stars and flaming torches. At the sound of the drums the tempo rises into a frenzy of movement around a huge camp fire with *kankurangs* and *kumpos* adding to the excitement.

In late 2006, Makasutu reached agreement with ten surrounding communities to expand these original programmes into one of the largest and most innovative sustainable tourism projects in Africa. The next decade will be just as amazing as the last at Makasutu!

Signposted off the main road at Kembujeh. Tel: 774 3322, www.makasutu.com. Open: daily 8am–5pm. Sat evening cultural spectacular beginning at 8pm (must be pre-booked). Admission charge.

Serrekunda

When Bathurst reached a certain size it could not expand any further because

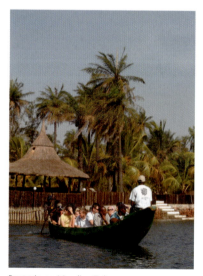

Boat trip on Mandina Bolong

THE LEGEND OF MAKASUTU

When English and Williams first discovered this land it had not been settled or farmed for centuries. Makasutu means 'sacred and deep forest' in Mandinka, and a local legend stated that the head of an illustrious tribal leader had been buried here after he was slain in battle and his spirit was protected by *djinns* who drive away any prospective settler.

The pair were undeterred by the legend, vowing to preserve the essential essence of the place, and the spirits seem happy with what's been achieved. It was only after the eco-attraction came to fruition that they heard of another Mandinka legend – that of two white men who would come to save the forest and make it famous!

of the restrictive Tanbi Wetlands Complex mangrove swamps that blocked its landward boundaries. Gambians looked for a location to create a satellite community and found it to the south inland from the coast at Serrekunda, then a minuscule and insignificant farming village. Today, where Banjul can claim to be the capital, perhaps the brains of The Gambia, Serrekunda is certainly the country's heart. Over 20 per cent of the population live here and the place pulses with energy at all times of the day. Every morning before dawn many thousands of people stream out of Serrekunda to work in Banjul or the Kombo resorts. Your tour guide or your wait staff will most likely live here, as do the bulk of the government civil service.

Serrekunda is not exactly a town or a city. As with many things in The

Gambia, the urban area simply grew organically, and several extended 'villages' are now glued together in a seemingly endless maze of dirt streets and alleyways, where thousands of family compounds stand cheek by jowl, cut by major thoroughfares that funnel traffic in a never-ending traffic jam of inefficient exhausts and old diesel engines.

The town has no museums or other real tourist attractions – it's the sheer weight of human existence that makes it a must for all visitors who want to understand what really make this country tick. This atmosphere is most palpable at the daily market – the largest in the country – where fish, fowl and kilos of seasonal vegetables are bartered, bought and sold. It's much less a tourist attraction than Albert Market in Banjul

(*see p33*) and foreign visitors may be bowled over by the scale of the place and the merchandise on offer, be it a replacement aluminium cooking pot, a goat or a hand-stitched linen shirt. There's a small craft market at the heart of the market where prices (negotiable) are lower than in the capital.

Market corner of Mosque Road and Sayer Jobe Avenue. Open: daily 8am–7pm (some stalls close 1pm Fri).

Tanje

Tanje (also spelled Tangeh and Tanji) sits on the south coast at the current boundary of the tourist strip. The new Sheraton Resort is only a couple of kilometres to the north, which will definitely change the atmosphere in the village in the next few years. Until then, Tanje is a touch of reality in contrast to

The sandy beach at Serrekunda

A weaver at work in Tanje

the settlement of Kololi where tourism overshadows everything else.

The Fish Market on the waterfront in the heart of the settlement is the largest in The Gambia. Several rows of permanent open-fronted counters are supplemented by impromptu beach stalls where the ladies drive a hard bargain to get the best price. As in the rest of the world, fish is becoming an expensive option, but you can't get fresher than this as catches are landed throughout the day. While it's the men that do the fishing on their 8- to 10-men pirogues, casting their nets and lines by hand, the heavily laden baskets and buckets are unloaded by hand by slender girls no older than 18.

North of the village centre is Tanje River Bird Reserve, a 6sq km (2sq mile) tract of land bounding the Tanje River which was The Gambia's first dedicated bird reserve. The beauty for 'twitchers' is that in this seemingly small area there's a whole range of habitats, from mangrove swamps and tidal flats to coastal woodland and sand dunes, so it attracts a vast range of birds, both native and migratory. Included in the reserve are the Bijol Islands, the country's only offshore territory, where seabirds and turtles nest undisturbed by predators. Unlike Abuko, there's no trail here so access is much more difficult, which is good news for the birds.

Tanje Village Museum is a private enterprise set up by the man who was once curator of the National Museum of The Gambia in Banjul. His brainchild was to create a living museum of Gambian lifestyle so that visitors could see how the people lived and find out more about their habits and customs. 'Putting The Gambia under one roof' was how he succinctly phrased it. The small village re-creates a family compound – the kind you'll see thousands of if you visit 'up-country', the interior of The Gambia. You'll also be able to watch the weaver and the blacksmith at work, examples of small-scale craftsmanship that are both still thriving industries. The small museum on-site has several rooms with information about native flora and fauna created in conjunction with the Parks and Wildlife Management Service of The Gambia. Most interesting are the cases showing traditional plants and their uses. Further rooms feature traditional musical instruments.

You'll also find the Camel Safari headquarters at Tanje. You'll need to book as part of an organised tour, but the stately cruise down Tanje's beach atop this ship of the desert is a great experience.

Tanje Village Museum. Tel: 926 618.
Open: daily 9am–5pm. Admission charge.
Tanje River Bird Reserve.
Open: daily 8am–dusk. Free admission.
Camel Safari. Book through
a tour operator.

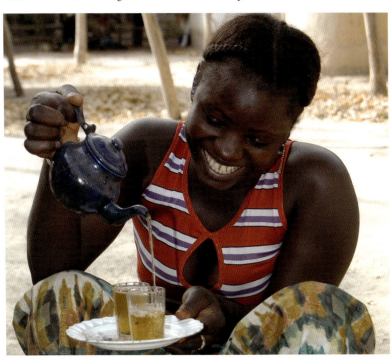

Time for tea at the Tanje Village Museum

Birdlife of The Gambia

Without doubt The Gambia is one of the world's best destinations for birdwatchers. Geographically it sits in a perfect location for migrant species that make the long journey from Europe to South Africa in the winter (returning north again for the summer), and the wide range of habitats it holds – from salt-estuary to riverine to woodland – attracts many different types of birds.

The Gambia's national parks protect healthy areas of pristine landscape

A great egret from the savannah

well away from the interference of modern human activity, but you'll be surprised just how many species you'll be able to spot even if you don't leave the 'tourist coast'. Take an early-morning boat trip in the Tanbi Wetlands Complex (*see p40*) to listen to the birdsong at dawn, or book time in a hide at Abuko Nature Reserve (*see p60*). Tanje River Bird Reserve (*see p56*) offers a wealth of options, while the Kotu stream is a great place for waterbirds. The areas of wasteland between hotel blocks can be a surprising source of birdlife, from hummingbirds to vultures, and herons and egrets can be spotted just about everywhere.

If you have an interest in birdwatching, you can book a specialised tour and hire a guide who'll be able to lead you to some rare and extraordinary birds (*see p157*). Scientists have documented over 500 species, and species counts of 250–300 are not unusual for the amateur during an average week here in the European winter.

What to spot
Here is just a handful of species you'll spot during a holiday in The Gambia.

A row of pelicans

Wetland species

African darter – a cormorant-like bird, sometimes called the snakebird because it has a long neck.

Whimbrel – the noisiest bird in The Gambia. The most widespread of the curlew family, it overwinters here in large numbers.

Pied kingfisher – a small, noisy bird with black and white plumage, it is numerous in *bolongs*.

Giant kingfisher – the largest kingfisher in Africa at over 40cm (16in) in height.

Pink-backed pelican – an African native.

Western reef heron – the most common heron in The Gambia, found in all wetland areas.

Goliath heron – the world's largest heron, standing over 1.4m (4^1/2ft) in height.

Freshwater river species

Blue-cheeked bee-eater – an overwintering species that adds spectacular colour to the sky.

Egyptian plover – also called 'the crocodile bird' because it can be seen cleaning decaying meat from around the teeth of these giant reptiles.

Senegal thick-knee – a resident breeding wader with large yellow eyes.

Savannah species

Beautiful sunbird – it's a delightful name, and this multicoloured bird can be found in hotel grounds.

Purple glossy starling – resident breeder and a numerous, gregarious bird.

Western plantain-eater – feeds on a range of fruits and seeds.

Abyssinian roller – brilliant plumage and around 30cm (12in) in height, these are insect feeders.

Palm nut vulture – whose favourite food is not flesh, but the seed of the palm nut tree.

Hooded vulture – a large scavenger often found by rubbish tips.

Great egret – largest of the species.

Walk: Abuko Nature Reserve

Abuko Nature Reserve, an exceptional tract of protected forest at the head of Lamin Bolong, offers one of the easiest locations to spot a range of wildlife. Try to visit early in the morning or late in the afternoon when the animals are more active. The path around the park is measured by regular markers counting up to 107. It's simple to follow and there are plenty of rest stops along the way.

You will find the services of a guide useful in identifying trees, birds and animals.

Allow 2 hours, or longer depending on wildlife-watching opportunities. Distance: 2.5km (1¹/₂ miles).

Once you enter the park, the forest closes in around the dusty track. About 200m (220yds) from the start of the walk you'll cross a riverbed on a narrow bridge.

1 Riverbed
This riverbed acts as a conduit during the rainy season, filling waterholes and allowing the park to provide fresh water year-round.

Another 100m (110yds) or so along the trail you'll catch your first sight of the watering hole, and then the Field Station on the right.

2 Darwin Field Station

This acts as a base for field scientists but it also provides excellent information for visitors. Climb to the observation deck for panoramic views across the watering hole where, at most times of day, you can spot crocodiles basking, plus a selection of wading birds – perhaps if you are lucky a deer might come down to drink or a monitor lizard might crawl through the undergrowth.

Just around the corner from the research station is a short route right to a hide at the water's edge.

3 Hide

This hide provides a close-up view of all the animals and birds that frequent the park. It's available for hire and is often used by birding groups. The best time to install yourself is before sunrise. *From here, it's a straightforward walk into the heart of the dense forest.*

4 Animals en route

Along the way you should encounter monkeys grubbing for roots or hiding in the undergrowth on either flank. You may also be lucky enough to see a duiker (deer) or a mongoose, both of which are more shy of humans.

At distance post 29 there is a shortcut path to the exit if you are already feeling jaded, but otherwise continue on. Marker 65 marks the furthest reach of the park and here you'll find the Animal Orphanage.

5 Animal Orphanage

It's a strange collection of animals in large but not particularly therapeutic cages. Most surprising are the hyenas with their impressive musculature. Another cage has a collection of baboons rescued from homes in The Gambia. Don't get close because some have developed very antisocial habits.

You'll also find a refreshment stall here with water and other cold drinks, plus a couple of craft stalls.

Leave the orphanage on the lane that runs to the right of the baboon compound. From here it's approximately 1.25km (³/₄ mile) to the exit where you'll find a small craft market. Or, if you've left a vehicle at the entrance car park, take the footpath right at marker 95, which leads back to the ticket office.

A shy deer may cross your path

Tour: The highlights of the tourist coast

The highlights of The Gambia's tourist coast are many, more than you could fit into one day. The attractions detailed here offer a varied itinerary with time to relax, shop and shake hands with one of nature's wildest creatures.

Allow 8 hours.

Distance: 58km (36 miles).

From the hotel strip at Senegambia, head north along Bertil Harding Highway to Bakua. Turn left at Kairaba Avenue and right on Garba Jahumpa Road for 1km (^{1}/$_2$ mile) until you reach Sait Matty Road. Once there, you'll need to ask for exact directions to Katchikally Crocodile Tank because it sits in a maze of dusty lanes and isn't signposted.

1 Katchikally Crocodile Tank

Katchikally is the most accessible of several sacred crocodile pools that are still used by local people in animist ceremonies. Tourists get to pet the somnolent beasts and have their photographs taken.

From Katchikally, ask for directions back to Sait Matty Road and return down Garba Jahumpa Road to Kairaba Avenue. Turn left here onto this long arterial thoroughfare and continue on until it meets Mosque Road. Turn right here, and at the end of the road (1.5km/1 mile) you'll find Serrekunda Market on your left.

2 Serrekunda Market

Serrekunda Market is the region's most interesting, in your face, African experience. Visit whether you want to buy or not.

From the crossroads where Mosque Road meets Sayer Jobe Avenue take a left and head south towards Brufut and Sekunda. After 4km (2½ miles) the road splits. Take the right fork and continue for another 7km (4½ miles), meeting the coast at Tanje. Once past the fish market you'll see a small sign for Tanje Village Museum on the left.

3 Tanje Village Museum

Tanje Village Museum offers 'The Gambia in one spot', re-creating a typical up-country village. The guides are helpful and knowledgeable.

From Tanje carry on south until you reach Sanyang (10km/6 miles), and in the centre of the village you'll find a tiny painted

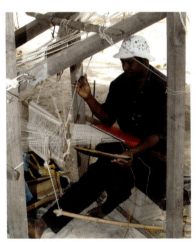

A weaver at Tanje Village Museum

sign on the right for Paradise Beach; this is a 3km (2-mile) dusty track, so take care.

4 Paradise Beach

Paradise Beach (Sanyang Beach) has a good beach bar, and you can watch the fishermen at work.

Return to Sanyang village and take the road east in the direction of Jambanjeli and Brikama. When the road reaches the crossroads at Brikama after 9km (5½ miles), turn left and 300m (330yds) along on the left is the craft market.

5 Brikama craft market

Brikama craft market is the best place to shop for wooden carvings. The articles are carved here so the range is good and the prices keen.

From Brikama, head north along the main road towards Banjul. When you reach the airport (after approximately 7km/4½ miles), take the left turn for the resorts and continue for 6.5km (4 miles) until you reach the small sign for Kombo Distillery on the left. Turn down the dusty track.

6 Kombo Distillery

One of the recent successes of the eco-industry that has sprung up in recent years, the Kombo Distillery is a Belgian enterprise, a 10ha (25-acre) fruit plantation that produces a range of excellent liqueurs. You'll be invited to a generous tasting session.

Return to the main road and turn left; cross the intersection and you'll return to the Senegambia strip in a few minutes.

Tour: The highlights of the tourist coast

The north shore

Separated from Banjul by the expansive waters of the River Gambia, the north shore offers a contrasting lifestyle that's easy to explore on a day trip from the coastal resorts. Some of The Gambia's most famous tourist attractions lie in this region and it's the centre of the 'slave' heritage trail that offers an emotional symbolic 'homecoming' for many African Americans.

Getting to the north shore is an adventure in itself. The Banjul/Barra commercial ferry crossing is a full-on slice of the push and pull of the daily grind African style, where modern 4WD vehicles vie for space with donkey carts, and foot passengers always carry more baggage than they can possibly handle. Crossing by vehicle requires a wait of at least two hours at any time of day. If you are touring independently it's much less time-consuming to take a taxi to the ferry at Banjul, travel across as a foot passenger and then contract another taxi in Barra to reach the attractions. If you do cross by vehicle, for safety reasons don't sit in your car seat during the crossing. Road conditions vary from excellent to terrible (the main road to Senegal being a case in point), but you can also reach many north-shore attractions by boat, offering a relaxing way to reach your destination.

Albreda

The slave trade along the River Gambia

was an international affair and the French administrated their operation from Albreda on the north bank, not far from Juffureh (*see p74*) and the English headquarters at San Domingo (*see p78*) and James Island, until the 1850s, one small anomaly of European international relations in that most complicated of centuries. Today the village is the landing site for boat trips on the 'Roots' trail, and visitors will make their way along the jetty to a re-creation of the 'Freedom Flagpole', so-called because if a slave could break free and touch the flagpole he would be allowed to go free. No records are kept to show how many actually achieved freedom this way, but there were instructions that any such prisoner would have to be branded with a certain mark so that if they were ever captured again, there was proof that they could not be taken into bondage.

The small garden around the freedom pole has displays of information about the origins of slavery and about the historical remains hereabouts. Gambians are not proud of the fact that there was a slave caste within its own society before the arrival of Europeans, but it was partly this acceptance of the concept of slavery by Africans themselves that allowed the colonialists to begin the trade that

would lead to grotesque exploitation on an unimaginable scale.

Looking out to the river from the Freedom Flagpole, you'll see ruined buildings to the left along the foreshore, now surrounded by a fleet of colourful dugout pirogues. Locals may tell you that it's a slave warehouse, but it's actually the CFAO trade warehouse dating from much later, in the post-slavery era.

Bao Bolong Wetland Reserve
The Gambia's largest protected area, the Bao Bolong (also spelled Bao Bolon) Wetland Reserve covers over 230sq km (89sq miles) on and around the Bao Bolong and a handful of other tributaries of the River Gambia flowing into it from the north. There's no permanent human settlement along the water's edge, leaving the area a pristine environment for native wildlife. The shoreline offers a wall of mangrove

The wetlands of the Bao Bolong Reserve

standing up to 12m (39ft) high in places, where some of The Gambia's final few manatees (sea cows) are said to forage, along with an equally small population of hippos and more numerous crocodile and clawless otters. North of the mangroves lie vast marshland and tidal flats, ideal for wading birds, while just inland from here is a sharp escarpment leading to tracts of dry savannah woodland. This is one of West Africa's richest bird environments, including occasional sightings of Pel's fishing owl and brown-necked parrots, and numerous African darters, Goliath and western reef herons and impressive fish eagles. The reserve has been included as a site of importance by the Ramsar International Wetlands Convention (*see box*) and in mid-2006 a bird viewing platform was opened, built with funding from the West African Bird Study Association (WABSA).

The park headquarters are situated at Dai Mandinka, south of the main highway and accessed from it via the village of No Kunda. Since there are no park maps or well-signposted trails, you are best advised to take a guide from here to make inroads into the savannah, where a handful of rural villages still consist of traditional round huts, or you can rent a dugout canoe to explore the *bolongs*.

Alternatively, you can access the reserve from the south bank of the River Gambia at Tendaba Camp (*see p90*). Although this won't allow you to step ashore and explore the inland environments of Bao Bolong, it's an excellent way to explore the mangrove and wetland scenery and its associated birds and animals.

100km (62 miles) upriver from the mouth of the River Gambia. Open: daily 8am–6pm. Admission charge.

Barra

This tiny bustling town is the northern docking point for the Banjul ferry and the foot and vehicle traffic feeds the economy. With car traffic queuing for at least five hours, and commercial traffic often waiting a week to cross, Barra makes a living catering to its huge temporary population at inexpensive street stalls and selling

THE RAMSAR INTERNATIONAL WETLANDS CONVENTION

Wetland environments have long been viewed as some of the most threatened in the world as river systems are 'managed' and land drained and claimed for farming. Ratified in Ramsar, Iran in 1971, the Wetlands Convention is a treaty of commitment to preserve wetland environments and provides governments with a framework for action within their own country while setting up an international forum of good practice, giving environmentalists access to expert advice. Over 1,600 wetlands have been listed as worthy of protection worldwide, covering over 145 million ha (358 million acres) in area (*www.ramsar.org*).

Barra Point

everything a Senegalese truck driver might need while he keeps a patient vigil before his turn arrives. The main approaches to the ferry dock are crammed with stationary traffic waited on by hundreds of youngsters offering peeled oranges, cashews and peanuts, and fresh water or fruit juice in single-portion plastic bags.

If you arrive in Barra as a foot passenger your exit from the port takes you through the town market. This is much more workaday then Albert Market in Banjul (see p33) but offers a fascinating picture of the kinds of merchandise that constitute the necessities for Gambians and Senegalese on the move, including vast quantities of plastic razors, jellybean sandals and small teapots used to brew up Gambian style (see p18).

Fort Bullen

The docking station is still protected by the sturdy bulk of Fort Bullen, built by the British as a counterpoint to the fort at Bathurst during the early 19th century in order to block French and Portuguese slave-running in the years after it had been abolished in British territories. Still complete with its round corner turrets, it saw service again in the Second World War, the remains of an anti-aircraft gunning placement that was installed at the time can still be seen, and sometimes plays host to Gambian army manoeuvres today. The huge river navigation beacon

DOG ISLAND

When the Portuguese first began exploring the river in the 15th century, they heard the loud barking of what sounded like huge dogs emanating from this small islet close to the north shore. Though a little frightened at the thought of coming face to face with a vicious carnivore, they made landfall to find that instead of dogs, the call was in fact the warning sound made by baboons who felt threatened by their approach. However, the name Dog Island remains to this day.

installed in the inner courtyard does somewhat spoil the atmosphere, but there are excellent views of the channel from the battlements.
Fort Bullen: Open: Mon–Sat 9am–7pm. Admission charge.

James Island

There are few pieces of land on earth so intimately connected with the slave trade as this islet replete with baobabs in the middle of the Gambia River. Between 1651, when it was founded by the Duke of Courland, and 1829, when the fort was abandoned, Africans were packed like sardines into the holds of cargo vessels and shipped like cargo to the Americas to work as slaves on the cotton and tobacco plantations. Between 1731 and 1740 over 26,000 slaves were documented as having been 'exported', but estimates suggest that hundreds of thousands met this same fate, their last view of their homeland being the ground of James Island. Most would never see Africa again.

The fort, James Island

Looking out through Fort James' battlements

Even if the historical era holds little interest for the visitor, it's hard not to feel the human story as you clamber onto the rickety wooden jetty to reach the island. The river is so wide here that it's difficult to see either bank. It must have instilled utter despair in the prisoners knowing it was almost impossible to escape and that their fate was sealed. The island is extremely small but was six times larger in 1651, the area having been eaten away by the force of the tides in the intervening centuries. Slaves were transported here from the north shore and kept in cramped cells for two weeks before finally being loaded on board.

The fort had 35 donjons, each with a capacity of 25 slaves, so maximum capacity was 875 individuals. The two-week interval between arrival and departure was usually enough to cause the weakest ones to die so they didn't take up ship space that could be devoted to a stronger specimen.

In addition to its job as a slave warehouse, the fort had a serious defensive role and was constantly harried by the French who also controlled tribal lands in the Senegambia region. They took the fort in 1695, 1702 and again in 1704, but each time it returned to British control. In 1719 the fort was seized by pirates and in 1768 it was attacked by Niumi forces, tribespeople who controlled the north bank around what is now Barra (*see p67*). One can feel a certain sympathy for the soldiers garrisoned here so far away from home and any semblance of normal society, and indeed the company did mutiny in 1708 when morale must have been at rock bottom.

Today, only the scant walls of the main central structure remain. There's one slave cell and a few sections of curtain wall, but the island requires extreme intervention if it is not to be lost completely in the next few years. UNESCO have added James Island to the World Heritage Site list, and one hopes that this will help to secure some kind of international help.

Access by boat from Banjul or Albreda.
Open: daily 8am–6pm.
Admission charge.

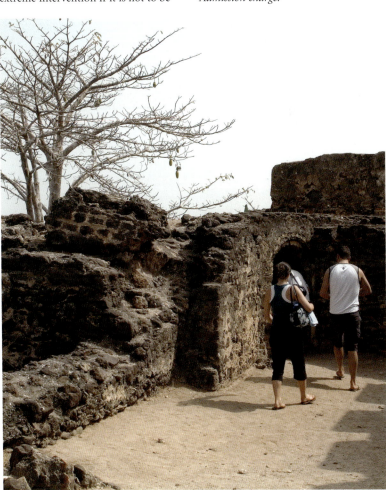

Exploring the ruins of James Island fort

The colonial slave trade

A severe shortage of labour in the 'New World' was the initial catalyst for the slave trade. The indigenous people of the Caribbean and South America had been swiftly wiped out by cruelty and disease but the cash crop system that made the colonies profitable needed a large number of strong farmhands. Arab traders and African tribal leaders in Western Africa were 'selling' men, women and children and the colonists made the decision to 'buy'.

Monument outside the Slavery Museum in Juffureh

The first slaves were reported in the New World in 1502, with numbers reaching a peak in the 1840s. At the height of the system, thousands of Africans were being shipped every month. Definitive numbers are unknown, but the minimum agreed by scholars is ten million individuals. Almost 6 per cent are thought to have been despatched from the region of Senegambia (Gambia, Senegal, Guinea-Bissau and Guinea). The journey was a brutal one. Captains expected that at least 25 per cent of their human cargo would die during the crossing.

The 'triangular trade'
A well-plied route linked slave countries, colonies and European ports. The three-leg journey became known as the 'triangular trade'.

Boats departed south from Europe to Africa carrying bartering beads, cloth, weapons and rum. When they reached Gambia, captains would sell or barter these for slaves. Once the hulls were packed with this human cargo the ships departed on the ten-week transatlantic crossing to America and the Caribbean where the Africans would be sold into slavery at markets in the port. This

A mural depicting slaves

freed up cash to be spent on fresh cargoes of rum, molasses and sugar – later cotton and tobacco – to be transported back to Europe.

The beauty of the triangular trade system was that boat owners could make massive profits on each leg of the journey, not having to wait until the ships finally reached home-port again. Because of the possibility of one single ship going down in the drink, or being lost to pirates or an enemy, it was normal for investors to have part shares in many ships, thus spreading the financial risk.

Abolition

The slave trade was abolished in the British Empire in 1807, but this related to the taking of any new slaves not the owning of any existing ones. Ironically, after the British abolished slavery, the trade expanded as the French and Portuguese fed demand via a 'black market'. In Gambia it was necessary to build a fort at Bathurst, now Banjul (*see p32*) and Fort Bullen (*see p68*) at the mouth of the River Gambia to stop foreign shipping traversing upriver to take Africans from under the very noses of the British. The owning of slaves finally became illegal in the British Empire in 1834. In Gambia, McCarthy Island was declared a refuge for freed slaves and a number returned to Africa to begin a new life on their native soil.

Effects on Africa – food for thought

British adventurer Archibald Dalzel (1740–1811), who served as governor of Ouidah, Benin, suggested that Africa could cope well enough with the losses of several generations of healthy men and women, whereas Walter Rodney (1942–80), a Guyanese historian, claimed that slavery is directly responsible for Africa being underdeveloped to the modern day. A question to ponder as African nations demand an apology from their old colonial overlords.

Juffureh

This tiny village was an insignificant farming settlement until 1976. Today, it's one of the most famous locations in Africa, courtesy of *Roots: The Saga of an American Family*, a book that galvanised African American society and put The Gambia on the international map.

When Alex Haley named Juffureh as the native village of his ancestor Kunte Kinte, the first of his line to be sold into slavery in America, the family and village had little inclination of the attention it would receive. Juffureh sits inland only a few minutes' walk from Albreda (*see p64*), with James Island (*see p68*) only a short boat trip offshore, so it has always lain close to the story of slavery. But before very long hundreds of people, many African Americans searching for their own family roots, began to arrive to walk the dusty paths in Kunte Kinte's footsteps. Today, visitors of all creeds and colours are still coming.

The Kinte family still reside here, though the mud and straw huts they lived in have been replaced by brick compounds. The knowledgeable official guides have plenty of background information about the slave trade in general and the Kinte family tree. The matriarch of the family takes time to sit with visitors, answering questions through an interpreter. You can also purchase an informative booklet explaining the background to the book with biographical details about Haley and the impact of the book on the African American population in the USA.

The Slavery Museum at Juffureh – officially the National Museum (North Bank) – does a far better job than its Banjul counterpart, and there's a wealth of information about this inhumane trade, why it happened and how the whole system worked. Housed in Maurel Freres Building, a trading post built in 1840, the information is presented in a straightforward manner, never leaning towards the judgemental, but in a way this only adds to the impact on visitors as the full horror of what took place on 'the voyage of no return' begins to sink in. The rusting manacles, yokes and chains show the brutal treatment meted out to the captives, while official documents listing totals 'exported' and numbers dying before transportation or during the voyage make very sombre reading. There's a model of the fort on James Island (*see p68*) as it looked in its heyday, which needs to be held in the memory when you set eyes on what now remains.

The final gallery in the museum offers an uplifting twist on the story of slavery. Entitled 'Portraits of a New Generation', it features photographs and short biographies of African Americans who have thrived in the USA and without whose contribution modern America would be a much poorer place (not only financially but also spiritually and morally). Positive stories of influential politicians such as Condeleeza Rice (American Secretary of State) and Marc Morial (Mayor of New Orleans); musicians such as Queen Latifa and Wynton Marsalis, plus a hundred or more sportspeople, businesspeople and scientists are highlighted, showing the rich talent bequeathed to the nation by the

generations of slave men and women who arrived powerless on American shores.

National Museum (North Bank). Tel: 226244 (Banjul). Open: Mon–Thur 10am–5pm, Fri 10am–1pm. Admission charge.

Kinte Family Compound. Open: daily 8am–6pm. Donation expected for any photographs taken.

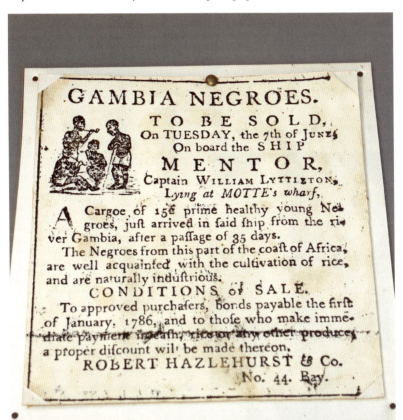

A poster exhibit at the Slavery Museum, Juffureh

The *Roots* phenomenon

In 1976 the publication of *Roots: The Saga of an American Family* captured the imagination of a generation of African Americans. The story of Mandinka warrior Kunta Kinte, kidnapped from Gambia in 1767 and sold into slavery in the USA, and the subsequent generations of the Kinte family – all ancestors of the story's author Alex Haley – showed African Americans that their history was not an anonymous one. The novel was an instant hit in the USA and was subsequently published worldwide in 37 languages. A TV mini-series screened in 1977 was avidly watched by 130 million viewers.

Roots prompted many African Americans to undertake detailed searches for their own genealogy, but just as importantly, the journey from the United States to The Gambia made by Haley became a pilgrimage undertaken by many more from all tribal backgrounds – the Kinte clan became symbolic kin of millions of American tribal ancestors, and a trip to tiny Juffureh became an emotional homecoming.

Recently, doubts have been thrown on whether this tiny village is exactly the ancestral home of a man named Kunte Kinte. Several authors have pored over Haley's research and found fault with the dates and locations. Some have even suggested that the *griot* Haley came to see at Juffureh in the early 1970s had been coached with answers that would please the visitor – little realising the chain of events that this would set in motion. But what is without doubt is that even if Haley was mistaken, misdirected or deceitful, the power of the *Roots* story is in no way diminished.

Alex Haley in his US Coastguard days

Entrance to the Roots Heritage Trail

Alex Haley

Alex Hayley was born in Ithaca, New York, in 1921, and his family moved south when he was a child. In 1939 he joined the US Coastguard. During long voyages he would alleviate the fear and boredom by writing stories and discovered he had a talent for it. After the Second World War, Haley transferred to the journalist division of the Coastguard where he worked until he earned his retirement in 1959. He then began a new career, writing full time.

Haley's first significant piece appeared in *Playboy* in 1962 when he interviewed legendary jazz musician Miles Davis about, among other things, his attitude to racism. This led to a theme throughout the 1960s where Haley would interview leading African Americans, including Dr Martin Luther King and Mohammed Ali. In 1963 Haley interviewed Malcolm X (African American human rights activist) and this meeting led to the writer being asked to ghostwrite X's autobiography. The resulting tome was said by *Time Magazine* to be one of the most important non-fiction books of the 20th century.

In 1966 Haley began research on a more personal story, the search for his 'roots'. This journey led him through several generations to Annapolis, Maryland, site of Kunte Kinte's arrival on American soil, then across the Atlantic to Juffureh, from where his family were said to originate. He won the Pulitzer Prize for his efforts.

Haley was working on a second genealogical novel, *Queen*, when he died of a heart attack in 1992. At his request the story was completed by David Stevens, an American actor.

Niumi National Park

Named after the Niumi peoples who traditionally occupied this region and the government district of Niumi that administrates the area, Niumi National Park protects coastal wetland environments that stretch all the way up the northern Gambia coastline from just north of Fort Bullen (*see p68*) to the Senegal border. It's only a stone's throw from Banjul but it's a little-explored park, at the heart of which run the sinuous curves of Massarinko Bolong, a waterway that sees few people. There are no public transport services to the landward side and it's not yet on the overland tour-group itinerary.

Niumi is a favourite location for migrant birds with a high overall species count, but most don't spend much time here. It's a vital pit stop down the African coast and they take a few days to replenish fat stocks before carrying on north or south depending on the season. However, there are plenty of native heron and ospreys and the savannah forests are known for their warblers.

A few manatees are said to live in the waterways but you'll be very lucky to spot one; more frequent are dolphins, especially in the dry season. Crocodiles and monitor lizards also call Niumi home.

Jinack Island on the western boundary of the park is the most popular destination for day-trippers, but the title is misleading. It's only cut

THE ROOTS TRAIL

One of the most popular day trips run by tour operators is the 'Roots Trail' which usually includes a lazy ferry trip from Banjul along the Gambia River with stops at Albreda, the National Museum (North Bank), also known as the slavery museum, the Kinte family compound to meet Haley's descendants, then a visit to James Island before the boat comes back downriver to the capital. You'll take lunch on board and hopefully catch sight of the playful family of dolphins that live in the expanse of the saltwater estuary.

You'll be '*toubab*-ed' incessantly from the moment you make landfall by children large and small, with pleading eyes asking for your empty plastic bottles (to carry drinking water to school) and hundreds of potential pen pals seeking to press scraps of paper with neatly printed names and addresses into your palm.

off from the rest of The Gambia by the width of a *bolong*. At low tide Jinack beaches stretch for 10km (6 miles) and the interior of dry forest is ideal birdwatching territory. Most of the island is in Gambian territory but the 'straight-as-a-die' border drawn up in colonial times cut off the upper point, which is now firmly Senegalese.
Northeast of Barra. Open: 8am–6pm. Admission charge.

San Domingo

Less then 1km (1/2 mile) from the centre of Juffureh, but little visited by modern tour groups, lie the remains of San Domingo, site of the first Portuguese settlement in Gambia which was taken over by the British and served as the departure point for Fort James.

Here the slaves captured by African tribesmen would be handed over to the British in return for weapons and goods. As with many historical buildings on the Roots Trail, very little remains at San Domingo, merely one corner and buttress of the old British trading station, but it's worth treading the path from here to the river, the final few steps slaves would have taken on their mainland soil. The path leading to the ruins is surrounded by farmland and free-roaming placid cattle. You may catch sight of families of monkeys tearing through the undergrowth. *Open access. Free admission.*

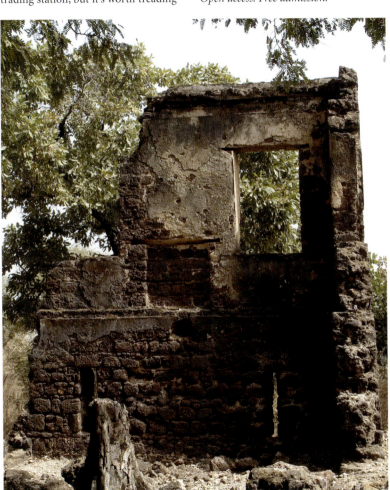

The ruins at San Domingo

Janjangbureh (Georgetown) and the mid-river region

The mid-river region brings visitors face to face with The Gambia's true African roots. Hectares of dusty deciduous savannah form the country's arable heartland, with tiny thatched rural villages continuing the practices of old. The vistas are incredibly beautiful and the people too, the smiles genuine and the interest in rarely seen tourists sometimes overwhelming but never threatening. The mid-river also introduces West Africa's mysterious ancient past, startling evidence of a history never recorded but certainly sophisticated – a society that we may never fully understand.

As the River Gambia narrows the further inland you travel, so do the country's boundaries, sometimes extending only a few kilometres either side of its banks. There are still only two crossing points west of the Banjul/Barra connection, and, although sharing a common nationality, for the most part the north- and south-bank communities have little contact with each other.

The southern highway is in a diabolical condition. Asphalted by the British, it has seen little repair since the colonial era. Resurfacing and expansion are taking place at the western end but it will take at least five years to complete the whole route, even if today's pace is maintained. Most travellers take the easier north-coast road, which is a shame, as the lack of traffic makes the south-route

settlements much more fascinating – you'll find kids playing football on this supposedly arterial road; monkey families congregate for a spot of mutual preening; and snakes warm themselves on the last remaining patches of black tarmac in the early mornings. Half of the north-coast route is now smooth, fast asphalt, allowing you to speed on through but miss the rural life just outside the window.

At the moment these are your choices for trips upriver, for aside from occasional bespoke cruises (usually at the end of the tourist season and before the rains start – *see Tour p92*) there is absolutely no east/west river traffic to take you up to Janjangbureh.

Farafenni

This north-shore settlement is a constant hive of activity because it sits on the trans-Gambia highway close to the ferry crossing at Bambatenda/Yelitenda and on a direct route with the Senegalese capital Dakar and its southern Casamance district. With the Gambian customs post in the heart of town it's a town where commercial traffic gets bottlenecked, so it's quite well stocked with eateries, and even has

a couple of basic hotels – an ideal stopover if you want to break the journey up-country, or spend some time at Bao Bolong Wetland Reserve (*see p65*) to the west.

The town holds one of the largest *lumo* (country markets) in The Gambia. Every Sunday the whole district travels to town to buy and sell everything from cattle to machine parts at what turns into an open-air commercial jamboree. Those without mechanical horsepower arrive on the back of fleets of donkey- and horse-drawn carts, transformed into public transport for the day. In addition to local fresh produce and livestock, you'll find traders from surrounding countries – French-speaking Malians, Guineans and Mauritanians – who sell all kinds of consumer goods including fabrics and clothing. You'll be able to explore and browse here without the pressure to buy that's sometimes felt at

A ferry docks at Janjangbureh

the tourist markets along the coast, though there's far fewer of the mass-produced souvenir items here. Try to time your visit for the *lumo* day if you can.

Janjangbureh (Georgetown)

Janjangbureh is a backwater in the modern Gambia, but for many years the town was a rival to Bathurst and the second city of The Gambia colony.

The town sits on mid-river McCarthy Island, leased from the local tribal chief by the British in 1823. They founded a fort and town named after the then monarch George III. Capital of the Central River Division, the local people would have you believe that the history of Janjangbureh is as inextricably linked with colonial slavery as James Island (*see p68*) and Juffureh (*see p74*) in the

west closer to the river's mouth, but the story is a little more mundane. The town was founded after the British abolished slavery, and in many ways its *raison d'être* was to enforce that edict, not to defer it. The purpose of Georgetown was to protect the eastern boundaries of the British Gambia province from French troops in Senegal and to found a base from where missionaries could spread the Christian word. In fact Wesleyan Protestants arrived here, to found their only church in West Africa. The island became a safe haven for freed slaves, the Akus, and those who escaped French and Portuguese incarceration. Farming was established and the fledgling settlement thrived.

Renamed Janjangbureh in 1995, the town is a full 300km (186 miles) upriver from Banjul. There's been very little investment in infrastructure since Independence, and this is a world away from the busy and relatively cosmopolitan capital. Perhaps Janjangbureh feels slighted by the loss of its influence; one might even suggest that it succumbs to malaise, but that would be an injustice to the vibrant day-to-day activity that brings the streets to life.

Janjangbureh offers the most easterly crossing point of the River Gambia, but the ferries here cannot support any heavy goods traffic. Two push-pull boats attached to wire hawsers – one on the north bank of the island, one on the south – carry a maximum of two vehicles and a contingent of 30 or so passengers on each crossing.

Trade was one of the main industries in Georgetown, and the north shores of the town still have the shells of immense late 18th-century and early 19th-century warehouses, the Maurel & Prom building and the CFAO building that serviced the river traffic, and both would certainly make superb boutique hotels and restaurants for the modern tourist market, were the investment available. A local guide might sit you down with stories of how slaves were imprisoned in these sturdy structures, but these are too young to be slave warehouses. That is not to say, however, that before the founding of Georgetown, the hunting and transporting of slaves didn't take place from these river banks; the trade was too insidious and widespread for it not

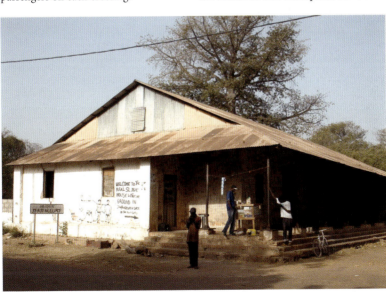

The Maurel & Prom building

to have happened, but it is necessary to state that these particular buildings played no part in it.

One block inland from the wharf, the Commissioner's Office building betrays a style of 19th- and 20th-century utilitarian colonial architecture. The outposts of the British Empire didn't benefit from many architectural masterpieces and this building is devoid of any flourishes and frills.

The Wesleyans founded a mission school in Georgetown, which soon gained a reputation as the best in Gambia colony. In 1927 it was renamed Armitage School and became the school of choice of the growing class of Gambian elite, motto 'Enter to Learn, Go Forward to Serve'. Immaculately uniformed boarders can still be found here, but the international schools in Banjul now offer serious competition.

In the heart of town is a small, well-tended park with a sapling baobab in the middle. Known as the Freedom Tree, it is said that slaves who freed themselves from bondage and touched the pole could not be transported to the Americas. Perhaps this tree, reminiscent of the flagpole at Albreda (*see p64*), was symbolic of the fact that the whole area of Georgetown was free territory to anyone escaping French clutches. The sapling was planted to replace a mature, colonial-age baobab that was damaged in the 1990s.

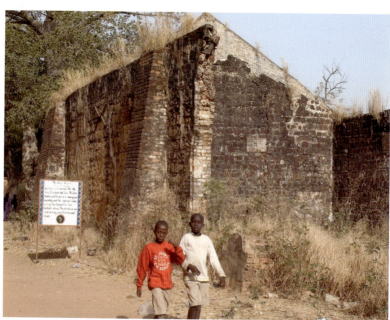

Ruined colonial warehouses in Findlay Street, Janjangbureh

Janjangbureh is surrounded by some exceptional freshwater riverine and savannah landscapes, with a biodiversity that is attracting the attention of scientists and tourists alike.

Kanilai

This small rural village has seen something of an improvement in its fortunes in the last 15 years. It's the birthplace of President Jammeh, and his family still manage the large farm where he spent his childhood years. The family compound has developed into a kind of second seat for the President and his cabinet, and he often entertains foreign guests here.

For most of the year, visitors must be content with touring the Kanilai Game Park, where an eclectic mixture of African animals forms the basis of what, in the long term, will be a conservation programme for species under pressure elsewhere on the continent, though few are native to The Gambia. You can enjoy impala, wildebeest, ostriches and zebra, plus a breeding pair of rhino. Less rare are the crocodiles, which congregate in large numbers around the freshwater pools. Access to the park is by vehicle only, accompanied by a ranger. Both ranger (and vehicle if you don't have one) can be hired from nearby Sindola Lodge (*see p156*), a luxurious place to stay by up-country standards.

Kanilai comes alive with Jola dancers and Gambian wrestlers during the International Roots Festival (in June)

An old wooden house in the centre of Janjangbureh

and other traditional get-togethers. The tourist office will be able to provide details of dates.
Kanilai Game Park. Open: daily 7–10am, 5–7pm. Admission charge.

Kerr Batch Stones

Though not as famous as the Wassu Stones (*see p91*) that draw the crowds, Kerr Batch Stones do get the occasional tourist group. The site is fenced and has a guardian ticket seller; however, during the rainy season the family grows crops around the stones, and if no visitors are expected they'll allow their cattle to graze the parched stems. A series of seven or eight circles comprising thigh- to chest-height thick circular stones, the Kerr Batch circles are not the most visually impressive, but they do have one rare

A cow inspects the Kerr Batch Stones

feature – a 2m (6^1/$_2$ft) high double *menhir* (standing stone) or lyre stone, which looks like a giant V-for-victory two-fingered salute. Scientists still have no clue as to why the ancients should have erected a double stone; suggestions are that two important people may have died within a short space of time and were commemorated together. However, this is another mystery that may never be solved.

The compound also has an interesting museum with many artefacts relating to the tribal practices of the rural area. Local beadwork, musical instruments and domestic tools have a real impact, because if you travel the dirt roads linking the rural villages you see the very same items in daily use. The landscape around Wassu has some wonderful arable savannah dotted

with tiny settlements complete with *bantaba* and dozens of smiling kids. *Signposted from Nyanga Bantang. Open: 9am–5pm. Admission charge.*

Kiang West National Park

One of The Gambia's least-visited national parks, the animals and plants of Kiang West currently benefit from the dire condition of the main route south of the river, meaning most travellers forging up-country tend to use the faster north route. It's a pity, because the park has some excellent tracts of pristine savannah and deciduous woodland, with healthy populations of all the country's major land mammals including bushbuck, duiker, noisy baboons, hyena, caracals and warthogs (known here as bush pigs). If you don't get the chance to see bush pig in the flesh – they travel in large, noisy family groups – you'll be presented with signs of their recent activity all around the park as they root through the mud and earth in search of roots and tubers, leaving behind metres of ploughed terrain.

The River Gambia forms the northern boundary of Kiang West, where, as with most riverine parks in The Gambia, mangrove rules. Many naturalists come to catch sight of the secretive sitatunga, an antelope that's made a home in the salt marshes and river shallows, and it's still possible to see the endangered manatee.

Kiang West has several escarpments from where it's possible to get overviews of watering holes or valley floors. Vehicular access is limited and exploration involves trekking on foot along several well-worn footpaths. The best vantage point is at Tubabkollon Point (*tubabkollon* means 'white man's well', so-called because the Portuguese founded a small trading station here) on the river in the northeast corner. This is an area where many of the land and mangrove animals mix together; however, it's quite a trek from the main road. Many visitors make a base at Tendaba Camp (*see p90*) and take a boat or walk into Kiang West from there with an expert guide to point the way. It's a 15km (9-mile) round trip on foot, but setting off early and making a day of it offers some great animal- and bird-spotting opportunities.

You'll have a lot of the Kiang West National Park to yourself

Access off south road 125km (78 miles) east of Banjul. Open: daily 8am–6.30pm. Admission charge.

River Gambia National Park

It is interesting that many of The Gambia's most successful and acclaimed 'eco' projects have been brought to fruition by the willpower

A mahogany tree beside the River Gambia

THE STONE CIRCLES OF SENEGAMBIA

Little is known about the ancient peoples of The Gambia, but what is certain is that their most obvious legacy proves them to be capable of social organisation. Over 100 sets of megalithic stone circles and many hundreds of *menhirs* (standing stones) dot the landscape up-country, spreading into Senegal to the north. Each one has been designed and erected with great care, but to what purpose remains unclear. Most don't make it onto the tourist maps but they fascinate archaeologists and anthropologists searching for clues about our African ancestors. So little is known about their origins that dates for their erection range from 1500 BC to AD 700 – this is one of the great unsolved mysteries of our age. All the circles comprise at least ten stones.

They could herald the coming of the rainy season (very important in this part of Africa), simply mark the passage of time, or pinpoint the burial place of important tribal leaders; artefacts found during excavations include spear tips and precious metal, suggesting a sacred place or perhaps the place of interment of a high-ranking individual.

All the stones are hand-cut from deep brown igneous rock found all over this vast region, so they were not transported across vast distances. But they did have to be shaped and manoeuvred into place, which required a great deal of time and application.

and sheer 'bloody-mindedness' of a few maverick individuals. Think of Eddie Brewer at Abuko, and English and Williams at Makasutu, for example. The same is true of the River Gambia National Park, a protected tract of watercourse surrounding the Chimpanzee Rehabilitation Project. This programme was started by Stella Marsden (daughter of Eddie Brewer) in 1969 in response to the number of captive animals confiscated during a purge on the ownership of these wild apes by authorities in The Gambia. The project founded three independent chimp communities on small, uninhabited, mid-river islands, free from the pressure of predators and other primate species. Currently over 70 animals form the study group, being monitored regularly by Marsden herself or by teams of visiting project workers. Other than that, there is little human contact.

Tour boats ply the river from Janjangbureh (*see p80*) a couple of hours upriver, and you may be lucky to spot chimps in the trees at the water's edge, or you can book a specialist stay at the Visitor Camp (*see p156*), where you can interact with the project workers and follow their work (though you cannot make footfall on the islands or meet the chimps themselves). You can also adopt a chimp if you want to provide financial help to the project.

Interestingly, some of the last hippopotamus populations along the river have begun to find a home in the safe waters of the park. It's thought that up to 100 of these huge river dwellers are still found within Gambian territory, but they spread along much of the upriver stretch and they are elusive.
280km (174 miles) upriver from Banjul.
Chimpanzee Rehabilitation Project
www.chimprehab.com

Janjangbureh (Georgetown) and the mid-river region

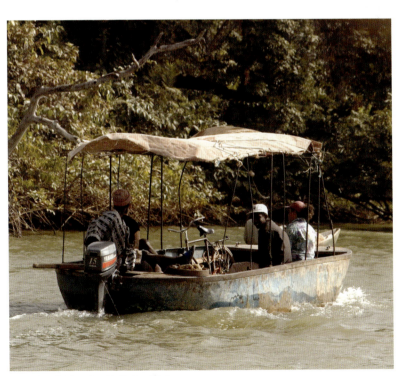

A tour boat in River Gambia National Park

Soma

Farafenni's counterpart of the south side of the river, Soma isn't as large or as 'fast paced' as its northern rival, being little more than a couple of intersections flanked by cheap food stalls, truck-repair shacks and petrol stations. It's a good place to stock up on snacks for the continuation of your journey.

Tendaba Camp

Tendaba means 'big wharf' in Mandinka, and this simple jetty is one of the very few landing points along this stretch of the river. Set on the edge of Tendaba village is Tendaba Camp, a mecca for birdwatchers and naturalists who use it as a base for explorations of the parks on both the north (Bao Bolong – *see p65*) and south (Kiang West – *see p86*) banks in this region. The overnight accommodation is basic, but it's a place for like-minded people to sit together in the balmy evenings swapping notes and discussing tomorrow's programme. There's a restaurant and an atmospheric little bar by the water's edge. You can join a group on a set itinerary or hire a boat and explore at your own pace. There are more than a few knowledgeable guides at Tendaba who'll help you get the best out of exploring wild The Gambia.

Tendaba. Tel: 554 1024. Open: daily.

Bush rooms at Tendaba Camp

The many circles of Wassu Stones

Wassu Stones

The finest set of ancient stone circles in West Africa, Wassu Stones form the largest complex of monumental structures in The Gambia and are impressive, not for their gargantuan size but for their number and the overall beauty of the site. More than 100 stones make up a series of ten or so circles. Over 80 of those are still standing in various small sub-sets of circles, each with a diameter of around 2m (6½ ft). The stones are slender and more graceful than those at Kerr Batch (*see p85*), most standing above 1.5m (5ft). One circle outranks the others in size with a series of well-carved monumental *menhirs*; however, this does not seem to sit in any position of authority within the site as a whole.

The compound has a small museum explaining how the circles were physically created. If you travel as part of a guided tour, you'll have a musical accompaniment to your trip as a couple of young *balafon* players play traditional tunes.

At Wassu you should leave a small stone atop one of the large standing stones to ensure good luck.
Wassu village. Open: 8am–6pm. Admission charge.

Boat tour: Upriver to Janjangbureh (Georgetown)

The River Gambia is a totally underutilised resource, both for transport and for tourism. It's the perfect conduit for exploration because nothing is very far from the water.

Unfortunately, not many boats offer the service, but one company, Jane's Boats (see p154), will run group trips at the end of the main tourist season and before the rains begin. The large double-decker pirogue can be your hotel and restaurant along the route. You'll sleep on deck under mosquito nets – how much closer to The Gambia could you be?
Allow 4–5 days.
Distance: 300km (186 miles).

1 Oysters
Take to your boat, and depart from Denton Bridge along Oyster Bolong. Then turn left along Turnbull Bolong to get your first view of the vast expanse of the lower reaches of the River Gambia.

Look out for oyster harvesters here, who work in the mangrove roots where the oysters develop, cutting them free with machetes. As you reach the river, you'll see Banjul city to the left.

The boat will then turn inland (east). As you pass Dog Island, look out for dolphins in this stretch of the river; they'll probably come to investigate the boat. After four or five hours' sailing you'll put in at Albreda.

2 Albreda
Here you can follow the Roots Trail. Learn about the slave trade and meet the Kinte clan – said to be the direct descendants of Kunte Kinte, ancestor of author Alex Haley (see p76). As you leave Albreda you can sight James Island, departure point for thousands of slaves shipped to the other side of the Atlantic.
Your boat continues pushing upriver and the banks will slowly begin to come closer together. It's a full day's sail to the next stop at Tendaba Camp.

3 Tendaba Camp
Tendaba is a world-renowned birding centre in close proximity to two exceptional national parks, Kiang

West and Bao Bolong. You can rent a smaller boat and take a guide to spend the morning exploring the maze of narrow *bolongs*.
A few hours further east, if it's Sunday make a stop at the Yetilenda/ Bambatenda ferry jetty and take a taxi to Farafenni.

4 Farafenni

The country market or *lumo* held here is one of the largest in the country and a fantastic cultural experience.

East of the ferry, the river begins to meander across a wide flood plain. Here the forest really begins to come into its own with lush mangrove and high stands of riverine forest. The birdsong is bright and varied, vying for air with the barking of baboons and other monkey calls, and there's little human activity.

Below the town of Kuntaur lies Baboon Island, a major eco-project.

5 River Gambia National Park

A collection of several mid-river islands makes up the River Gambia National Park, which is home to the Chimpanzee Rehabilitation Project. You'll not be allowed to land on the islands but you may spot chimps on the banks. The national park also protects a small population of hippos.
After the national park, the boat plies on, rounding a major bend at Kuntaur before the final turn to Janjangbureh.

6 Janjangbureh

As Georgetown this was Britain's eastern colonial outpost and a haven for freed slaves. Now it's a sleepy town set among magnificent riverine ecosystems.

Boat tour: Upriver to Janjangbureh (Georgetown)

Walk: Janjangbureh (Georgetown)

Georgetown once rivalled Banjul in importance. It was Great Britain's upriver command post from the 1820s and was a vital administrative and trading settlement. Set on mid-river McCarthy Island, it became a haven for freed slaves after the British abolished the practice in their empire.

Allow 1 hour. Distance: 1km (¹/₂ mile).

Start from the jetty of the vehicle ferry at the northeast end of the town.

1 Vehicle ferry jetty
Vehicular access to McCarthy Island can only be achieved by these characterful push-pull ferries with a capacity of two or three cars or one large truck. Spending an hour or two people-watching at the ferry dock allows you to watch the ebb and flow of daily life up-country.
Walk up the concrete jetty to where it meets the road. To the right stands the remains of the Maurel & Prom building.

The vehicle ferries can only take a couple of cars at a time

2 Maurel & Prom building
A large and dour warehouse built in the late 1800s, the Maurel & Prom building is not old enough to have had any connection with the slave trade. However, you may be approached by a 'guide' who will regale you with stories of cruelty and imprisonment.
Walk straight on past the building and after 50m (55 yds) you'll reach an intersection. Just ahead, slightly to the left, is a small triangular garden with a young sapling at the centre. This is the Freedom Tree monument.

3 Freedom Tree
The legend of the monument says that any captive that broke free from his shackles and touched this tree could not be taken into slavery. Because Georgetown was surrounded by hostile enemy territory – that of the French who still worked the slave trade – the town literally ensured freedom for any African who could swim across to the island.

Continue on inland past the Gamtel office, then turn first right at a dust road.

4 Commissioner's Offices and Residence

On the left here is The Gambia's high-security prison, while on the right are the remains of the Commissioner's Offices and Residence. Once the most prestigious building in the town, the shell is now badly neglected.

Walk on down the lane, and after 170m (190 yds) you'll reach the campus of Armitage School.

5 Armitage School

Inaugurated in 1927, the school catered to colonials and the Gambian elite; it still attracts boarders from around the country.

Retrace your steps back to the Maurel & Prom building. With your back to the building, walk down Findlay Street, which lies straight ahead.

6 CFAO building

The vast façades of the buildings on the left overlooking the river belong to the CFAO buildings, a rival set of colonial warehouses to the Maurel & Prom, and much more elegant in their form, though still only bare skeletons of buildings.

Continue down Findlay Street, and after another 150m (165 yds) the street turns sharp right.

7 Wesleyan Methodist Church

On the right here you'll see the simple form of the Wesleyan Methodist Church. This was the only outpost for this small Protestant denomination in Western Africa, and the Wesleyans were an important element in the early success of Georgetown.

At the end of the road here turn right on Owen Street to find yourself back at the Freedom Tree, then turn right to the ferry jetty.

Organised tours in The Gambia

There are many possible tours you can take whilst in The Gambia, whether your interest lies in the natural environment, the wildlife or the everyday lives of the Gambian people.

BOLONG TOURS

Creeks known as *bolongs*, bedecked with mangrove, form by far the most common natural ecosystem along the river, and you really haven't been to The Gambia unless you've spent some time on the water surveying the mass of tangled brown roots and verdant mantle. *Bolongs* are a vital resource for native birds and animals and hundreds of species of visiting birds. Under threat around the world, the mangrove ecosystems in The Gambia are becoming increasingly important for their pristine nature.

The tourist coast

In the Kombos you can join a group boat tour of the *bolongs* of the Tanbi Wetlands on a large double-decker pirogue. Early starts are best for birdwatching because, around dawn, there's a lot of activity as roosting birds wake. Of course, not everyone is interested in species counts and spotting a rarity, but it's surprising how many people who've never thought about visiting a bird reserve get hooked when on one of these trips.

But birdwatching isn't the only reason to book a tour. Take an afternoon cruise for a spot of sunbathing on deck with the breezes cooling the air, or book a special sunset trip with cocktails and canapés to simply enjoy the views and the tranquillity.

Bolong trips from Makasutu Cultural Forest (*see p52*) take place in dugout pirogues powered by small engines that seat around six to eight people, so you sit much closer to the water and get much more of a feel for your surroundings. As part of a day of activities, you'll enjoy a 30-minute itinerary on the water, but visit as an individual and you can negotiate a longer and more detailed tour.

You can rent kayaks from Denton Bridge Watersports (*see p149*) at Denton Bridge, to power yourself into the *bolongs* of Tanbi – though you'll have a guide so you don't get lost. These smaller craft allow you much closer access to the banks and smaller tributaries, and you can dictate your own pace. The centre also has wave runners, but do be aware that travelling at high speed on these craft will create waves that can disturb birds and other life on the shore margins. Use them as a vehicle for stealth rather than as an instrument of speed.

Upriver

Up-country, *bolong* trips are a totally different affair. From Tendaba Camp (*see p155*), the *bolongs* of the national parks at Kiang West and Bao Bolong are within easy reach and the ecosystems are so much more varied than along the coast. Here the trips don't take a couple of hours but last up to a whole day, taking you to places little visited by humans. Only a small number of visitors to The Gambia make it up-country and usually in small groups, so small craft and pirogues are the norm.

You also have the option of hiring a pirogue for a private visit where, once again, you have the advantage of dictating the pace and locations you want to visit. This will give you maximum opportunity for, perhaps, hippo or clawless otter sightings. Your guide will be able to take you to the most likely locations and you can spend as much time as you want once there.

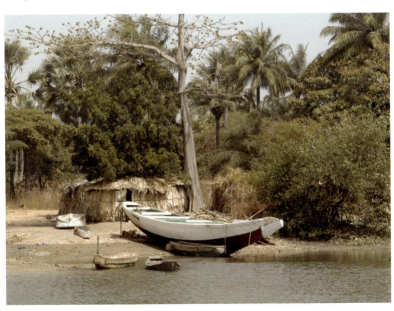

Pirogues moored in Mandina bolong

BUSH SAFARIS

Not the grand journeys across open treeless plains in search of big game that you find in Kenya or South Africa, cross-country or bush safaris in The Gambia are much more low-key, but no less enjoyable. Take a cross-country trip from your coastal hotel, book a vehicle and driver to head up-country or take to the trails on foot. There's a lot to see.

On the coast

On the coast, most tour operators run cross-country excursions in sturdy old army trucks, with seating in the back,

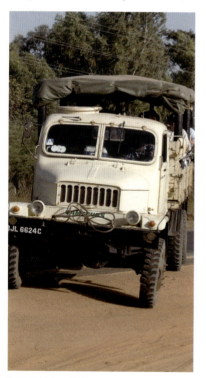

Tour group in a 4WD

which are ideally suited to the terrain. They traverse the dusty and potholed tracks with ease, and the high vantage point and open sides mean you get an excellent view of the passing villages and fields. Once off the main arterial route, the villages become remarkably rural very quickly, with family compounds clustered together and surrounded by small arable fields.

For a more sedate perambulation, take the camel safari from the base at Tanje village. These 'ships of the desert' take a route down the beach, in the shallows amongst the Atlantic flotsam and jetsam. It's quite a serene feeling once you get used to the movement; it's the getting up and down from ground level that can cause spills.

Tip

If you are heading out on a truck safari, take a fleece or a sweater because it can be cold for the first hour or so of the trip before the sun rises. Also, if you have long hair, take something to tie it back because it blows in the wind, and you'll never get a hairbrush through it after the trip.

Up-country

Up-country, although The Gambia is a small country, the landscape is big, with plains of giant baobab and silk cotton trees with a proliferation of deciduous forest and tall grassland spreading out north and south of the river. There are no black-top roads here away from the major highways.

This is a fascinating area to explore, though it's wise to hire a 4WD vehicle and engage a guide if you don't want to spend hours lost along the way. Routes range across dried seasonal lake-beds or through grassland savannah, and the dust can be very debilitating during the dry season, but the rainy season can see routes turn into a quagmire of clawing red mud which makes travelling more difficult.

The national parks up-country have limited vehicular access, but knowing these routes can make journeys on foot to find wildlife a lot shorter.

Trekking cross-country is really the only way to get to certain useful vantage points such as Tubabkollon Point in Kiang West National Park, or the bird hide at Bao Bolong. Kiang West is easily reached overland from Tendaba Camp in two or three hours, and exploring a park at walking pace allows you to follow up every rustle in the undergrowth or tweet in the canopy. Be prepared with sturdy shoes, comfortable clothing and a hat. Don't forget a decent pair of binoculars or a scope, and take water and snacks because there is no provision at all in the parks.

VILLAGE VISIT

For anyone who wants to learn more about the culture and lifestyle of the peoples of The Gambia, there's nothing

Organised tours in The Gambia

Baobab trees in the savannah

more illuminating than a visit to a village. Though the building methods may vary from concrete in the west to mud and thatch in the east, most villages work on the same social system.

Each village has several important locations that can also act as a social meeting place. For men it is the *bantaba* – a large wooden or metal bed or couch usually placed under the largest silk cotton tree in the village for ample shade. Here the men spend many hours discussing the issues of the day.

The village well is a focal point for the women. The Gambian authorities have worked hard to provide villages with modern hand-pump systems, which have made life easier. The women need to fill containers at least once every day, or take washing to be pummelled and pounded, and it's a

A village woman and her children cleaning rice

great opportunity to pass the time of day and have some fun.

The mosque is, of course, the spiritual centre of the community, with Friday lunchtime being when all the men of the village gather together to pray. Mosques are often very humble buildings, but perhaps the only one in the village built in brick or concrete.

If you visit the Sifoe Kafo Farm, a beekeeping co-operative at Sifoe near Brikama, you'll then go on to visit one of the family compounds of the women who work there – exactly which one is chosen by lots at the time of your visit, which is pretty egalitarian – and you'll be welcome to explore the family home. During the day the family, usually two or three wives with several children, live outside. A couple of *bantabas* serve as seating and food preparation areas. You'll be invited into the simple buildings that serve as bedrooms. Each wife has her own room, while the children sleep together. Behind the sleeping quarters are the animal shelters, one for the fowl and another for the goats and sheep.

Be sure that wherever you decide to get out of your vehicle, you'll be surrounded by a group of young children shouting '*toubab*' and trying to take your hand as you stroll, asking quick-fire questions like 'What is your name?' and 'What is your country?'. Most will want a little something – be it your plastic water bottle, a pen or some sweets. It's difficult to give to one without a flood of others assuming you have an unending supply of whatever you've given away. Still, you have to remember how little these children have and, especially up-country, how exciting it is to be given even small items that are a rare commodity in the local community.

SCHOOL VISIT

Schooling is not compulsory in The Gambia, though the government recommends that all children over the age of seven receive some kind of formal education. Many families are too poor to send their children to school, but with the country hoping to springboard into the 21st century it is imperative that this latest Gambian generation be able to take advantage of any opportunities presented by Jammeh's dreams for his country.

Without resources, many schools are poorly equipped to drive this change, and a visit to a local school, either

Schoolchildren in Juffureh

Children gather to sing for visitors

privately or with a tour group, brings home the great divide in educational provision between the developed and developing world. Books and materials are scarce and classrooms more so. Many early-stage classes have 100 pupils, while older children usually share lessons with 50 others. Pay for teachers is woefully inadequate when compared to cash-easy jobs in the tourist industry, though there are many dedicated individuals trying to make a difference in the education system. The education of girls is seen as a primary aim. Girls are often kept at home while boys receive what little education a family can afford, but women are the primary carers for young children and are therefore important role models.

All the major tour operators have 'adopted' a local primary school to be included in their 'cultural' tours, and you'll be allowed to visit the classrooms full of smiling pupils; they may even sing a welcome for you. Many people take materials such as books and pens (though pencils are better because you can rub out work and use books again, where ink leaves a permanent mark), and repeat visitors are often well prepared with old textbooks, maps and posters. The pupils learn in English, so anything designed for the UK National Curriculum, including resources produced by commercial companies, will be welcomed. Visitors without resources usually leave cash, but of course it's very difficult to monitor where the money goes once you leave the school compound.

The SOS Orphan School in Banjul is also featured in many tour itineraries.

It's a marked contrast to the government-funded schools: well-dressed kids in classrooms full of books, posters and smart new desks, there are even TVs with video players to enhance the learning experience. What has to be remembered is that most of the children here are without the traditional family support system that's so important in The Gambia, so they need the solid start in life that SOS can provide. Remember also that because SOS is an international organisation, any donations you give will be accounted for in a professional manner.

Some visitors feel so moved by the obvious lack of educational opportunities in The Gambia that they form a very personal relationship with a given school, raising money and organising the delivery of regular supplies of paper, pens, pencils etc. But what is certain is that no matter how often visitors are moved to help individual pupils or individual schools, education has to be one of President Jammeh's most pressing long-term issues.

Organised tours in The Gambia

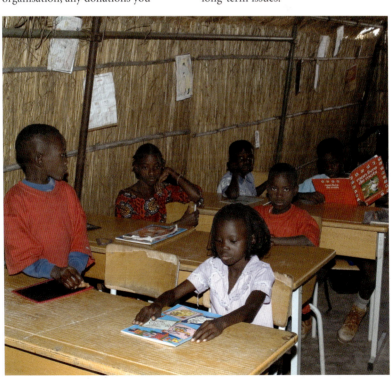

A typical bush schoolroom

The animals of The Gambia

Though the range of animal species found in The Gambia isn't as impressive as its tally of birds (see p58), with only 108 cited mammal species, the possibilities of easy viewing of several exotic species far outweighs the lack of variety.

You don't need to venture too far from the hotels of the Kombos to encounter endearing troops of monkeys. The Gambia has large numbers of vervets, colobus and red patas that frequent the grounds of the large hotels and wait for handouts of peanuts. Monkeys are easy to spot at Abuko, and there's a small unofficial Monkey Park close to the Senegambia Hotel where the inhabitants are pretty tame.

Larger and more belligerent are the baboons that range the countryside in troops. The infants and juveniles are as cute as the monkeys but the large dominant males can be aggressive and shouldn't be approached.

The shoreline and the river
Fiddler crabs are by far the most common shoreline creatures, sifting the mud banks for nutrients. In the water, look out for Atlantic humpback dolphins that roam the straits between Banjul and James Island.

Rarer species often only seen on tours into the national parks are clawless otters, hippos – which are now though to be only around 100 in number – and manatees (sea cows), water mammals related to the elephant, now very rare but still inhabiting the mangrove shallows.

Inland
Up-country you find the ubiquitous monkeys and baboons along with a healthy population of warthogs (a wild member of the pig family), which live in family groups called 'sounders'. Equally abundant are squirrels, and antelope species such as the duiker.

Less numerous and not so easily seen are hyena and caracal (a lynx-like wild cat). One animal never seen by the casual visitor is the leopard. Although it is said to inhabit The Gambia, numbers are unknown and sightings are rare.

By night
By night, bats are king. Smaller species are the tourist's friend because they eat masses of mosquitoes, but the largest is the fruit bat, also known as the flying fox, which plays an important role in seed dispersal. Bush

babies inhabit the nocturnal world at Kiang West (*see p86*), but you'll need a specialist guide to find them.

Reptiles

In addition to crocodiles, The Gambia has some fantastic reptile species; in excess of 74 have so far been documented. The monitor lizard can reach over 2m (6$\frac{1}{2}$ft) in length and is most easily spotted on the river banks or around waterholes. There are 41 species of snake, including the spitting cobra, the green mamba and the carpet viper. The most common lizard is the agama, but you could also see geckos and chameleons.

FEEDING THE MONKEYS

The authorities in The Gambia are trying to dissuade visitors from offering food because in the long term it may cause monkeys to lose their fear of humans and they may develop a dependency on the handouts rather than hunting for roots, fruit and nuts in the wild. It may be worthwhile discussing these issues with your children before they get caught up in a situation where they will just ache to offer a peanut or two.

The Gambia is a great place for spotting lizards

Getting away from it all

Tourism is highly developed in the far southwest corner of the country and there is a reasonably well-worn tourist trail east to Janjangbureh. East of McCarthy Island, however, you really are off the beaten track.

THE FAR EAST OF THE GAMBIA

In this continental corner of The Gambia society is 100 per cent agrarian, with small villages scattered across the countryside, where women tend the fields while the men chew the fat on their shady *bantabas*. It couldn't feel further away from the bustle and push of the coast. This is a flavour of the true heart of Africa.

Bansang

An unremarkable settlement, but famed in birdwatching circles for the breeding population of red-throated bee-eaters that inhabit the walls of a nearby disused quarry.

Wind down with a spot of fishing

The area also has healthy seasonal populations of carmine bee-eaters.

Basse

The 'capital' of the eastern region, Basse is where the tarmac road runs out. There are no actual attractions but the vehicle ferry means it's a focal point for traffic and it's always busy. The town has been a centre of weaving and pottery for generations and you can watch the artisans at work and buy from roadside stalls around the town. Birdwatchers visit Basse for its healthy numbers of Egyptian plovers.

Fatoto

The easternmost town in The Gambia of any size should be visited for its 'end of the world'-type atmosphere. There's a *lumo* every Sunday, but other than that it's a sleepy little place.

MUNGO PARK

Born in Selkirk, Scotland in 1771, Park qualified as a doctor but also developed an interest in botanical fieldwork. In 1788 he founded The Linnaean Society (now the leading society in the world for the study of taxonomy) with his friend Joseph Banks.

In 1794, Park heard that an expedition to discover the source of the River Niger had stalled because of the death of its leader. He offered his services and was accepted as a replacement. Park arrived in Gambia in June 1795, and travelled 200km (124 miles) upriver to Pisania to recommence the project. On 21 July 1796 he reached the Niger at Segu, the first European to set eyes on the river. He charted the course for 300km (186 miles) before returning to Scotland at the end of 1797, when he wrote *Travels in the Interior of Africa*, a detailed narrative of his trip.

Park was invited by the British government to undertake a second expedition to find the mouth of the Niger and he departed for Gambia at the end of January 1805, reaching the Niger in August. Park set off downstream but was attacked by hostile natives and drowned at the Bussa rapids when his boat became fast on the rocks.

Karantaba

Karantaba is the nearest settlement
to what was once Pisania, a British
up-country trading post. It was from
here that Mungo Park set off with his
expedition to find and map the River
Niger. A simple obelisk on the river
bank outside the village acts as a
memorial to the explorer, who lost
his life on the river he discovered.
Karantaba hosts a *lumo* every
Wednesday, when the normally
somnolent streets come alive
with activity.

SENEGAL

Senegal is not only The Gambia's
closest neighbour; it surrounds
Gambian territory on three sides.

Many of the ethnic groups of
The Gambia also settled in Senegalese
territory, giving the two countries
many things in common – but the
colonial history of Senegal is very
different, being French territory
until 1960. Today, Senegal is
resolutely Francophone in its
outlook, compared to The Gambia,
which is Anglophone.

Tour operators in The Gambia
organise several trips into Senegal,
either for the day or for a night or two.
It's also easy to travel across the border
independently, taking a bush taxi to
the border and picking up another
one at the Senegal side (car rental
companies don't allow rental cars to
cross the border). Currently, the UK
government Foreign Office
issues advisories against travel to
the Casamance province south
of The Gambia, so all roads lead
north across the river.

Even a short trip into Senegal
highlights several stark contrasts
between the two countries. The
wonderful roads are the first,
with smooth, rut-free asphalt
linking all the main Senegalese
settlements. The second is the
temperature. The climate of
northern Senegal is influenced
much more by its proximity to
the hot and arid Sahara, and as
soon as you leave the cooling
effect of the River Gambia the
thermometer starts to rise.
Third and most obviously is

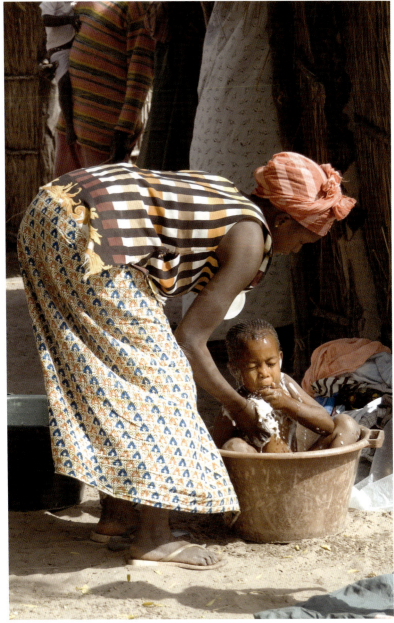

Bath time on Sipo island in the Saloum Delta National Park

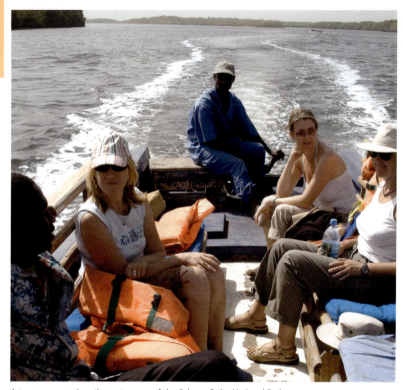

A tour group explore the waterways of the Saloum Delta National Park

the language. Though the ethnic languages are common to Senegal and The Gambia, the official language of Senegal is French, and English speakers are few.

Saloum Delta National Park

The closest town to the Gambian border is Toubacouta, a tiny resort with a couple of hotels set in the heart of the Saloum Delta National Park, a biosphere reserve of 76,000ha (187,800 acres). Sandy islands and masses of mangrove on the seaward boundary give way to deciduous savannah inland. Pelicans and flamingos are among the major draws, but the park also has populations of 36 mammals including manatees and dolphins.

Dakar

The Senegalese capital Dakar can be reached from The Gambia after a full day on the road. A city of one-and-a-half million people, it's a cultural centre of West Africa and the focus of Islamic pilgrimage. Recently the city has also become a musical capital for the *mbalax* rhythms that have taken the world by storm.

The Institut Fondamental d'Afrique Noire (IFAN) has one of the finest anthropological collections in Africa, with galleries of tribal masks, ritual objects and art from many African ethnic groups, plus one of the most complete archives in the continent, dating back to the early colonial era.

Gorée Island, just 3km (2 miles) outside the city, is Senegal's James Island, the final departure point for the New World for thousands of imprisoned Africans transported by both the French and the English. The buildings here are well preserved, from dour slave quarters to elegant mansions, and they house several museums including the Maison des Esclaves, Historical Museum, Fort d'Estrées and Musée de la Mer.

Senegal's La Porte du 3éme Millénaire (Third Millennium Gate) is the most recent change to the city skyline; it was finished in 2001. For shopping, Kermel Market is a great place to browse for souvenirs and is famed throughout West Africa for its fabrics and good-value local clothing.

View from Dakar across to Gorée Island

When to go

The Gambia has two main seasons – the rainy season and the dry season. The rhythm of life in the countryside is ruled by when the rains arrive and when they stop, and so, to a certain extent, is the tourist season. The climate of the coastal strip is influenced by the proximity of the ocean, while up-country the climate is swayed by the pressure systems at work in the heart of the African continent.

The dry season

The dry season starts in October and runs into June on the coast, but ends perhaps a month later in the east. Note that, though daytime temperatures vary little between rainy and dry season, the night-time temperatures drop quite dramatically in the dry season – enough for Europeans to need a light sweater while local Gambians pile on whatever warm clothing they have. As the name suggests, during the dry season there is very little rain and there is a subsequent drop in humidity and in mosquito numbers. As the dry season progresses the vegetation gets more and more sparse and dry, and the countryside takes on an almost sepia-tone hue, with parched leaves and dusty river beds.

The rainy season

From June to mid-October rainfall rises significantly. It isn't like a constant monsoon but it falls in hard storms, filling up the city streets and creating inland lakes up-country where rice crops

are quickly planted. Between storms, the sun shines as brightly as ever, sucking up the water, so humidity rises rapidly with the rains, and nights become hot and sticky. The number of mosquitoes increases and dirt roads become boggy messes, but, on the upside, crops grow

WEATHER CONVERSION CHART

25.4mm = 1 inch
°F = 1.8 × °C + 32

rapidly and the country is filled with beautiful wild flowers that in turn attract insects and butterflies.

When to visit

Most charter flights to The Gambia run from the beginning of November until the beginning of May, coinciding with the most lush period of the dry season, when temperatures are pleasant to warm and humidity is low. These are the best conditions for building up a tan on the beach or spending days in the national parks, birdwatching or animal spotting.

Christmas and Easter are the busiest periods, while cut-price flights and

THE HARBINGER OF THE RAINS

The mighty baobab has long been the farmer's friend. Throughout the dry season it stands bare and skeleton-like, but it comes into leaf just before the rains start – so new foliage heralds the imminent end of the yearly drought.

packages are easiest to find for the first few weeks or last few weeks of the season.

Between late May and late October, the tourist infrastructure almost closes down, so accommodation is difficult to find and few restaurants and bars are open.

The beginning and end of the dry season are good times to visit – warm but not crowded

Getting around

Getting around The Gambia is quite a challenge. With no internal flights, trains or upriver ferries, you are pretty much limited to horsepower, literally or figuratively, to get you where you want to go! The infrastructure is painfully in need of investment, with dire road conditions and a lack of road signs and decent maps. Patience is needed as cross-country journey times can be long, but local transport along the tourist coast is cheap, plentiful and relatively reliable.

Local taxis

These bright yellow vehicles, also called 'bush' taxis, are the basic form of public transport for Gambians. They come in all shapes and sizes from rusty old Renault 4s to 'new to The Gambia' minibuses, all with a capacity of 'however many can squeeze onto the seats'. Bush taxis run along set routes but pick up and drop off anywhere along this route. Passengers pay for the distance travelled plus for each item of baggage they carry, and fares are paid when you get off. Journeys are cheap and it's a great way to meet the locals.

If you don't rent a car or a car and driver, long-distance bush taxis are the only way to travel around up-country, but even then, they don't travel regularly to every settlement. You'll need to plan your journey or be flexible about exactly when and where you travel. Taxis are often laden with crops, and even animals, as well as people; tethered chickens along with goats and

kids are regular baggage. For long-distance journeys you'll pay before you travel, and fares and baggage fees are open to negotiation. If there are many taxis on the same route you'll be accosted by touts trying to get you into their vehicles, but be aware that bush taxis don't leave until full, so you may have a long wait if business is slow.

It may be quicker to hire the whole taxi to yourself – private hire – rather than wait until the taxi is full and have passengers being dropped off and picked up along your route. To find an empty taxi, you'll need to go to the taxi garage – normally near the market in towns – to negotiate a price.

One thing is for sure; there are reliability issues with bush taxis and you'll often see one or more broken down at the roadside with passengers waiting patiently for help to arrive. Breakdowns are just something else to factor into a road trip and seem to be accepted by Gambians themselves.

Tourist taxis

Bush taxis aren't allowed to enter some sections of the tourist coast, notably the Senegambia strip and Cape Point. A specially licensed fleet of green-coloured vehicles services the hotels. Tourist taxis are supposed to be more reliable, newer vehicles, and drivers have to prove they have insurance. The drivers also speak good English and can help with planning itineraries. Tourist taxis are more expensive than bush taxis (at least three times the price), but they offer return-journey prices with a certain amount of waiting time included so you can factor in time for a visit to an attraction or a meal out in the evenings. Prices are posted at the rank outside every hotel so there's no

TAXI ETIQUETTE

If trying to flag down a taxi, don't stick out your thumb as you would if you were trying to hitch a lift; this action is considered rude in The Gambia. Hold your hand out and wave it up and down. If the driver has capacity he'll stop for you, and if not he'll speed on by.

need for negotiation; however, if you want to engage a driver for the day, it pays to barter over the price.

Ferries

With only three crossing points and no bridges, the River Gambia presents an enormous barrier to travel, not just for Gambians but also for the Senegalese who must cross Gambian territory to reach their southern provinces. The two

Getting around

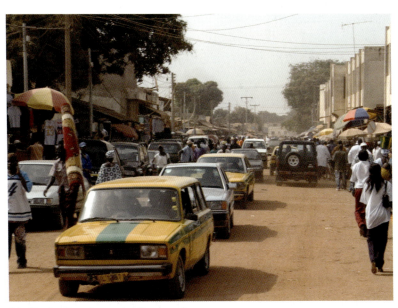

A taxi is often the only way of getting around

vehicle ferries crossing from Banjul to
Barra are the largest in the country, but
cars still have to wait at least four hours
to cross and commercial traffic up to a
week. The Yelitenda/Bambatenda ferry
is the second major fording point, with
a preponderance of Senegalese truck
traffic, while the tiny ferries at
Janjangbureh both take no more than
two cars each at any one time.

Currently, there are no ferries
carrying passengers up and down
the river.

Car rental

Car rental is not widespread in The
Gambia, though it is possible to have
one delivered to the hotel or pick one
up at the airport. The lack of street
signage and good maps makes
navigation almost impossible in the
Kombos, and the condition of the roads
and tracks up-country isn't for the
faint-hearted or inexperienced.

Hiring a car and driver by the day or
longer is much more common –
though if you are travelling up-country,

Ferry, Banjul port

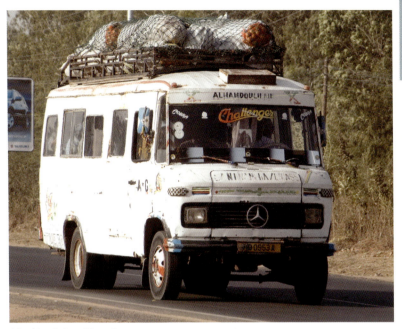

A local bus laden with produce

clarify who will be responsible for driver meals and accommodation before you start the trip. A third option is to rent a taxi by the day. This works out better financially if you don't intend to undertake excursions every day. You are then paying for a vehicle only when you actually use it.

When choosing a vehicle, think about the journey you are going to undertake. For many routes 4-wheel drive makes sense, and for up-country journeys something with 4-wheel drive and good suspension is advisable.

If you do decide to drive yourself, you should drive on the right and overtake on the left where possible, but be aware that, especially up-country,

drivers stick to the best possible road surface on any given stretch. Don't build up great speed on smooth sections as they don't last long and sudden hard breaking can be dangerous. Keep a watchful eye out for other road users, be careful of animals on the roads and potholes on the surfaces. After dark there is almost no street lighting anywhere in the country, so extra care is needed.

Travellers with disabilities

There are no specialised transport services for travellers with disabilities. Consult a ground operator such as Gamtours (*see p149*), who can help with the logistics.

Accommodation

The opening of the new Sheraton Gambia Resort Hotel & Spa at Brufut Beach in early 2007 has set a new benchmark for accommodation in The Gambia. A true five-star resort, it is by far the most luxurious hotel in the country and will spearhead a repositioning of The Gambia in the marketplace over the next few years.

The Gambia's tourist coast has a selection of accommodation in most price ranges. The earliest hotels do look a little dated with their block styling, but more recent builds have taken the setting into account and are much more sympathetic to the surroundings. There are no high-rise monstrosities blighting the beaches, but lovers of 1970s architecture will feel right at home. Most hotels are enhanced by verdant gardens, and there are choices in all price ranges that have direct access to the beach.

Hotels in The Gambia use the international star rating system for quality, but be aware that ratings don't always match quality ratings in Europe or North America and should be used for comparison with other hotels in the country rather than with hotels in other countries. Rooms are generally spotlessly clean in all categories, though at lower star ratings fittings may be careworn. Since the offshore undercurrents make swimming in the sea difficult, you may want to pay particular attention to pool size, especially if you have children.

All-inclusive packages (flight, room, meals and/or drinks) are an important part of holiday provision in The Gambia. This can represent value for money, but there is a good choice of eateries in the tourist areas for those who would rather choose a bed and breakfast rate.

In the last decade, the seeds of a new generation of upmarket eco boutique hotels have been planted here. These chic lodges make the most of their exotic location yet provide touches of luxury and personal service not seen before in the country, including room service and excellent food. They make fantastic romantic getaways and offer the chance of some quality 'me' time away from the crowds.

Up-country, in the east of The Gambia, accommodation is limited to a few unpretentious lodges. You'll sleep in concrete or mud-brick round huts such as at Janjangbureh Camp, or in strong canvas tents at Bird Safari Camp, which offer a bed, simple private facilities with toilet, sink and shower, and an evening meal. Some have plunge pools, but most simply represent somewhere to rest your head after a long day wildlife watching or travelling.

There is one campsite in The Gambia. Sukuta Camping offers simple accommodation such as you find at the up-country camps, but also has space for tents and motorhomes. It caters to the steady stream of intrepid travellers crossing the Sahara.

In all price categories, rack rates (walk-in rates) are high. The cheapest option, unless you can get a very cheap flight, is to book flight and accommodation together as part of a package with a major tour operator. One- and two-week packages represent excellent value for money and are discounted if there is late availability.

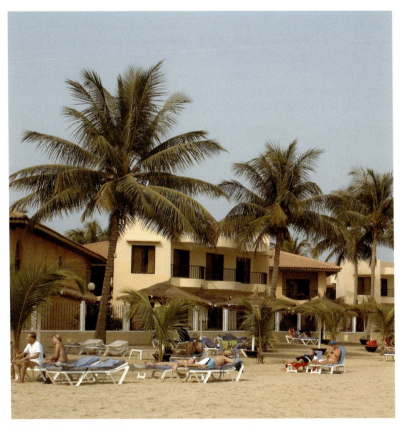

The Ocean Bay resort in Bakau

Food and drink

The mountains of fresh produce for sale in all the local markets are evidence of a robust local cuisine with some delicious dishes to try, but The Gambia doesn't have a book of set recipes. The staple dishes vary in the balance of ingredients depending on the season and the economic status of the family, but they are worth exploring.

Gambian dishes

The basis of all Gambian cuisine is to take a good serving of a filling carbohydrate mixed with or topped by a small amount of a rich sauce containing meat or fish. The main

Chillies for sale in Albert Market, Banjul

carbohydrate is usually rice, but couscous (tiny pieces of durum wheat) or cassava are also common. Popular sauces include *domoda* (a rich peanut sauce) or *plasas* (a palm oil and cassava leaf or okra sauce). *Benachin* means 'one pot' in Wolof and is a dry rice 'risotto'-style dish with varying amounts of meat or fish and vegetables.

OYSTERS

Oysters form an important part of the daily diet, but they aren't the kind farmed in Brittany or the south of France. Gambian oysters grow wild on the mangrove roots and resemble a European mussel in shape and texture. Only certain families are involved in harvesting oysters and it is women's work. After being cut from the mangrove stem the oysters are taken back to a shoreline camp and smoked while still in their shells. They are then opened and graded – very large for restaurants and hotels, medium for selling to the public, small for home consumption.

Nothing of the process is wasted. The shells are dried for two years then burned, pounded into powder and sold as whitewash for village huts.

Jolof rice is similar but cooked with tomatoes and vegetables. Chicken *yassa* is available just about everywhere. The chicken is marinated in an aromatic mixture of chilli, garlic and lime to create a strong and zesty flavour.

Meat

Chickens, goats and sheep roam free even in built-up areas such as Serrekunda, and families will eat these on feast days and during celebrations. Meat on sale in butchers is *halal* (killed in accordance with Islamic law). It's usually lamb or beef and it's fresh each day. The Christian community are the only ones to keep pigs, and they usually only service their own domestic needs.

Most meat served in hotels in the Kombos is imported because the country can't supply it on a large enough scale to service the needs of the tourist industry.

Fish

Fish is always a good choice because the catches are landed every day. Bonga fish is most popular with Gambians because it is cheap and plentiful, but it has lots of small bones so isn't to everybody's taste. More commonly on restaurant menus you'll find butter fish and lady fish, larger, more muscular fish with a firm texture. Bigger fish such as tarpon are also available, and prawns are farmed around Albreda. Try the delicious *bolong* oyster (*see left*) in a soup or stew.

A restaurant in Kololi

Drinks

Though most Gambians don't drink alcohol, The Gambia has its own domestic brewery, Julbrew, which opened in 1977 and makes very drinkable lager. The brewery also makes Guinness under licence.

King Kombo distillery supplies small quantities of delicious tropical liqueurs that are unlike anything else on the market.

Tea is the drink of choice in most Gambian homes, and the ritual of

---

TIPPING

Waiters will certainly appreciate a tip. Leave the small change at bars and around 25 dalasi at dinner unless you are at a top restaurant, where a little more is the norm.

Food and drink

The local 'poison' from JulBrew

Food and drink

ETIQUETTE

At home, most Gambians will eat with their hands and, because the left hand is the unclean hand, use the right hand only for touching food. If you are invited to a family meal at a compound you should also use only your right hand for taking and holding food.

making it is a time-honoured one (*see p18*). Hibiscus petals are also infused to make a hot or cold drink. Coffee is always Nescafé, served hot and strong.

Where to eat

Around the tourist coast there are hundreds of restaurants to choose from and they usually combine some Gambian cuisine with international dishes on their menus.

Once up-country, international-style restaurants are almost impossible to find, but the main commercial districts will always have one or two basic eateries serving reliable staple Gambian dishes. The bush camps all serve food, generally a buffet with the main dish being a Gambian one.

Snacks are easier to find. At major intersections and around markets you can buy bags of cashews or peanuts, juicy peeled oranges, steamed cassava stalks, or fried dough balls with hot chilli sauce.

Vegetarians

Vegetarians are rarely specifically catered for in The Gambia but can usually still find something to suit. Pasta dishes with meat-free sauces are usually included on the menus in restaurants along the tourist coast, but often even dishes one would assume free from animal products, such as vegetable soups, are made with meat stock, so ask before you order.

Tasting session at King Kombo distillery

Entertainment

The ethnic groups of The Gambia each have their own traditional tribal songs and dances that still perform an important function in modern life. Songs and dances relate to important rites of passage through life and celebrations marking turning points in the seasons. These thriving art forms offer visitors a rich vein of folkloric performances to enjoy.

The best place to see these songs and dances being performed is *in situ* in the villages up-country during celebrations and rituals, but cultural or folkloric evenings in the resorts do a reasonable job of bringing the flavour and energy to a tourist audience. Try to visit the evening performance at Makasutu Cultural Forest if you can, because the atmosphere and the setting are the most magical of all the commercial shows.

Traditional village dance display

Musicians playing the *kora* and *balafon*

Music

In Mandinka society, the rights of story telling and song are the sole domain of the *jeli* or *griot*, the traditional holder of the oral history. A *jeli* is called upon to perform at naming ceremonies, circumcisions and weddings as they have been for generations. They sing lilting songs illustrating the long history of the tribe and the family, vocals accompanied by the *kora*, a lute-type instrument made from a hollowed-out calabash with over 20 strings that is played with the strings facing the player. The repetition of simple refrains on the *kora* creates an almost Zen-like background sound and it is used in many hotels and attractions as an aid to relaxation.

Another very relaxing sound is that of the *balafon*, a xylophone-style instrument with wooden blocks of various sizes tied together between two stands that are tapped with wooden sticks to produce the sound. The deep resonance of the notes forms a base percussion canvas upon which the contrasting timbre of the *kora* and *riti* can paint a picture in sound.

The percussion is further beefed up by drums. Mandinka drums are traditionally three in number of varying sizes from large to small, but the big Wolof drums really pack a punch. It's a sound that fills the air and requires a lot of effort from the players themselves. The rather macho nature of drumming means that it's a popular pastime for young male Gambians, and you are bound to hear drum sounds booming through the air at least once every day during your visit. The most common drum played today is the *djembé*, which is made of a piece of wood hollowed out and shaped like an hourglass, with a taut goat skin stretched over one end, tied in place with cord. This skin is then tapped with the hand to produce the beat.

The *riti* is a Jola stringed instrument played with a bow like a violin, though the number of strings can vary from one to four. It produces a range of high-pitched sounds that accent the voices or the base notes of the drums and *balafon*. Similar instruments are the *kotingo* or the *bolom*.

Different types of flutes made from wood, bamboo, calabash or clay also add a high note – these may be substituted for a whistle in modern music displays.

Entertainment

An instrument that is making a comeback is the *akonting*, another stringed, lute-like instrument made from a dried calabash that was the forerunner of the Western guitar. The Akonting Centre for Senegambia Folk Music at Madinari village is a centre of excellence for this and other traditional Gambian music.

Mbalax music

One of the most popular and well-known genres of the modern 'world music' scene is the West African *mbalax*, which radiates out of Senegal but has several Gambian virtuosos. Here the *sabar* (Wolof tall drums) and *tama* (drum held under the arm) form the percussion soundtrack to the lilting reedy vocals of the *jelis* and the sound of the *kora*, but traditional West African

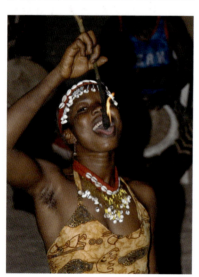

A fire-eating performance at Kololi Beach

sounds have been mixed with influences from the Caribbean such as *reggae* and *ska*. Youssou N'Dour is the most internationally famous *mbalax* musician, but there are many more to enjoy.

As *mbalax* itself has developed it has branched out into '*mbalax* rap' and '*mbalax* hip-hop', creating whole new musical tie-ups and yet more West African home-grown popular music.

Head to one of the market stalls selling CDs and tapes and ask them for *mbalax* music. You should be able to pick up sample albums for around £1 each.

Gambian dance

Most of the traditional Mandinka *griot* tales are for listening to, not for dancing to, but when it comes to the thundering beat of the drum solos, the dancers have something that fits the bill exactly.

A line or circle of clapping women builds the tension until one of them jumps into the sand lifting knee and elbows high in quick succession in rhythm with the drum strikes, pounding the ground with the heel on the down stroke. It's a high-energy movement that tires even the fittest dancer after 30 seconds or so, so as one dancer finishes, another steps into the arena to keep up the momentum. At its best the movement is so fluid that all you see is a puff of dust rising as the feet stomp down, and all else is just a blur of movement.

In Jola tradition male dancers also perform very physical movements, such as back spins and head spins, that have influenced the modern body popping, body patting and hip-hop moves.

Many cultural performances also include the appearance of traditional spirit guides like the *kankurang* with his coconut matting costume, and the *kumpo* with his costume of long rhun palm fronds with a pole pointing out of the top – both of which protect against the effects and presence of evil in traditional communities. Stilted dancers and fire-eaters also add a touch of the dramatic.

Bars/clubs and discos

There is a good range of nightlife on the tourist coast with Irish-style pubs, karaoke bars and clubs for dancing, and these are open throughout the season. At the latest hot spots, the crowd is swelled at weekends by young urban Gambians. Local clubs featuring recorded or live *mbalax* are always busy at weekends and are a great way to get into the West African beat.

The nights start late here and most nightclubs don't open before midnight; however, there'll be no shortage of places to enjoy a couple of drinks before that, if you want to start a little earlier.

A *kankurang* or spirit guide

Shopping

For lovers of local handicrafts, The Gambia is a shoppers' delight, offering an exceptional range of artisan-produced items for every budget. You are bound to find something to suite your taste. The best items are both practical and beautiful.

Basketware

Grasses have traditionally been used to create natural containers in a range of sizes and colours. Choose anything from bread baskets to linen baskets.

Batik and cloth

Batik fabric is another traditional Gambian handicraft and you can buy it as art or made into clothing. Hand-woven cotton cloth in traditional tribal patterns is fashioned into table runners, place mats or shoulder bags.

Beads and bangles

The colourful barter beads that the colonial Europeans traded for slaves in the 16th and 17th centuries kick-started a fashion for beadwork in Africa that continues into the modern age. Original beads are now expensive and very hard to find, though some traders will assure you that they have the genuine article. More common are inexpensive strings worn as chokers, bangles or anklets.

Fetish items or *jujus*

The treatments prescribed by animist tribal witch doctors to increase spiritual strength and fight evil spirits, such as metal bangles, and tooth and hair objects, have become such valuable collectables that originals are difficult to find. Still, tourist stalls will normally sell newer versions featuring cowrie shells, bone and metal.

Music and musical instruments

Small souvenir *djembé* drums are sold at just about every tourist market stall, but you'll also find good-quality hand-made full-size drums, *balafon* (wooden xylophones) and exquisite *kora* (stringed lutes) on sale. Tapes and CDs of Senegambian *mbalax* music make an excellent addition to your collection.

Wood carving

Wood carving is a tradition passed from father to son and it's The Gambia's most popular handicraft. The quality of the work is very high, it's simply a matter of finding something you like – from traditional tribal masks to crocodiles, elephants or decorative bowls. Traditional hardwoods such as mahogany or ebony are now almost impossible to find, so be aware that most dark wood carvings are dyed with shoe polish.

Where to buy

The Gambia's craft markets or *bengdulas* are the place to find a full range of souvenirs and compare price and quality. You'll find a *bengdula* at every tourist resort, or at Serrekunda market or Albert Market in Banjul. Beach stalls and hotel souvenir shops also have a good choice of objects.

HAGGLING OR BARTERING

Bartering or bargaining is a fact of life in The Gambia. It isn't something that comes naturally to a shopper who is used to fixed prices, so here are several tips to make the bartering process more successful and enjoyable.

To start with, look at several items and act cool about the specific item you want.

Your first offer should be around 40 per cent of what the shop owner asks, then increase your offer little by little. You'll probably end up paying around 50–60 per cent of the original asking price.

Keep smiling! This isn't a contest; it's a way of reaching agreement.

If you don't want to pay the price, simply tell the shop owner and walk away.

Once you agree a price it is very bad manners to change your mind!

Shopping

Bracelets for sale at Tanje Village Museum

Batik

Batik is the art of decorating cloth (usually natural cottons and silks) using wax and dye. It is practised in many countries around the world, each with their own ethnic patterns and images. The word batik originates from Java in Indonesia, where *tik* means 'to dot', and the technique in this Far Eastern country is to put the wax on the material by way of numerous taps of a pointed quill. The Portuguese were the first Europeans to see this technique outside Indonesia and simply imported the Javanese word to describe it. The technique in The Gambia is to use the quill to isolate large blocks of cloth, like a child colouring with crayons.

Batik artist at work

The raw materials

The Gambia always had natural beeswax in abundance and mangrove leaves were used as a natural mordant. The earth gave up a palette of natural dyes in the beige and brown ranges, plus a strong indigo blue much in demand in Europe, which helped to create 'serge de Nimes' or 'denim' (now synonymous with fashionable blue jeans). Today artificial paraffin wax is used more commonly in commercial operations because it's much more user-friendly. It melts at low temperatures and provides a longer working time before it solidifies, and artificial dyes may also be used because they provide reliable colour relatively inexpensively, along with a chemical mordant.

Lost wax technique

First the pattern needs to be planned on the fabric. Any whites to be found in the final finished piece are covered in wax by use of the metal 'quill', then the cloth is dipped in the first dye colour. Any element of the pattern to be kept the first colour is then covered in wax and the whole is dipped in a second, differently coloured, dye bath. To preserve elements of this second colour other sections are covered in

A finished piece of batik work

wax before a third colour is added, and the process continues and the colour range expanded to produce ever more elaborate designs. When the pattern is finalised, the whole canvas is washed in boiling water, which seals the dye and melts the wax. The whole process is ecologically sound because the wax can be reused numerous times.

Tie 'n' dye or 'tie dye'
A traditional technique throughout much of Africa and Asia, 'tie dye' puts pattern onto fabric by a process of resist dying.

Resist dying uses some kind of barrier between cloth and dye so that parts take the colour and parts don't. In the case of tie dye, the fabric is bundled together and parts are tied with a strong rope, or the fabric is knotted, before it is immersed in the dye. The fabric at the heart of the knot or rope bundle resists the colour most, while a round wheel of colour, running light to dark, is created as a final pattern. Subsequent processes complicate and deepen the pattern and the colour.

Traditional African ethnic patterns feature shapes and colours rather than 'pictures', but most batik found in the tourist markets along the coast are quite literal landscapes featuring rustic thatch huts, coffee-skinned maidens carrying loads on their heads, or bright beach scenes with swaying palms.

Sport and leisure

Organised sport and leisure activities are not well developed in The Gambia, since relatively few Gambians can afford to spend money on hobbies and pastimes. However, the tourist development along the coast has stimulated provision of a range of activities catering specifically for visitors and these are expanding all the time as the industry develops and matures.

SPECTATOR SPORTS
Football (soccer)

Football is a major passion with Gambians. Television coverage of all the major leagues in Europe is available for only a few dalasis a game at local bars and sports clubs, so you'll find favourite teams ranging from Arsenal to AC Milan, Barcelona to Bolton Wanderers. Almost every male Gambian between the ages of 6 and 25 wears a jersey with a player's name on the back – the modern uniform of youth – though royalties definitely aren't going back to the players and clubs for these endorsements.

Gambians are always happy to chat for hours about football and there are several minor amateur leagues for players, but the professional game isn't very well developed, so there's little chance of seeing a good live game. The best matches are held at the Independence Stadium in Bakau on Saturdays in the dry season. The national team is currently managed by German Antoine Hey but it makes no impression, even in the pan-continent African Nations Cup competition, when compared to the likes of Nigeria and Cameroon.

Independence Stadium

The huge, sparkling-new Independence Stadium in Bakau is a rather grand venue for all manner of sports and social events, including soccer cup finals and a few international matches. It also hosts the finales of parades and political rallies.

Wrestling

Senegambian wrestling, or *borreh*, is classed as the national sport. Until President Jammeh came to power, it was a dying art, but he has raised the profile and features it in most of the national festivals and events, so a few more young people are taking it up. It's not a sport that can be found on every street corner, however. The best time to see competitions is during

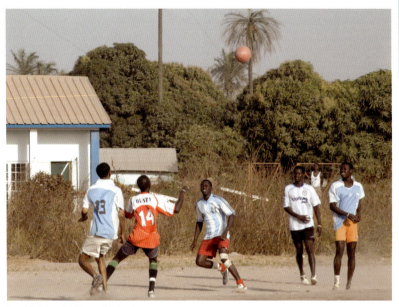

Local lads playing football in Tanje

diplomatic events held by the President at Kanilai.

The style is similar to that of Graeco-Roman wrestling, in which the combatants must try to throw their opponents through holds of the upper body only, rather than attacking the legs and lower torso. The contests can be ferocious and bloody, but, typically of any Gambian public spectacle, they have a theatrical backdrop with lots of drumming and tribal singing.

PARTICIPATORY SPORTS
Birdwatching

By far the most popular leisure pastime for visitors, beyond lazing around on the beach, birdwatching is one of The Gambia's main tourist money earners.

The country has several advantages over its neighbours in that it has a range of ecosystems that attract birds, and a collection of protected areas where their habitat is not under threat. Government-licensed guides are helpful and knowledgeable and you can hire them by the hour or by the day. Guides can supply binoculars but it's far better to bring your own if you have them. Specialist birdwatching trips are easy to organise either before you depart for The Gambia or during your stay, through a ground tour operator such as Gamtours (see p149).

Cycling

Cycling is one of the most pleasurable ways to explore the countryside of

Bicycle rental in Kotu

The Gambia. On the tourist coast, attractions are not great distances from one another and the landscape is flat. Once off the major roads there's very little traffic and you can travel at your own pace.

There are cycle rental kiosks in all the major resorts and you can rent by the day or longer. Not all bikes are in the best possible condition, so check brakes and tyres before you set off. Cycle helmets are not generally available, so if you have one at home, bring it with you.

Cycling is also a good method of touring up-country if you have the stamina. The southern arterial road inland is in such dire condition that cycling is probably the quickest form of transport, because you can steer around the potholes. This would make a great adventure if you were willing to stay in local villages on your travels.

Golf

There are two golf courses in the tourist area, though playing here is a little different to a round at home. Gambian course managers have long since given up on trying to irrigate vast tracts of countryside when water for crops can be in short supply, so 'greens' are 'browns' – and putting areas are kept impeccably by 'browns keepers' who rake and flatten them after every player has passed. Golfers 'drive' balls off rubber mats instead of teeing off from grass.

The Fajara Club is a long-standing ex-pat meeting place that, in addition to a par 69 18-hole course, also has tennis courts, squash and badminton facilities. It welcomes visitors (though you have to pay a temporary membership fee), who mostly visit for the golf.

The Kololi Beach Club also has a par 3 18-hole course. It's a part-ownership holiday complex that opens the course to day visitors.

Horseriding

You can rent horses at Kotu beach for sunset treks along the strand. The riding is not difficult so it's suitable for all abilities, but it's not particularly challenging if you are an experienced rider.

Sport fishing

The rich, cool Atlantic waters offshore from The Gambia attract large numbers of fish – as witnessed by the catches landed by the fishing fleets every day. Sport fishing targets the largest of these species including barracuda, stingray, threadfin salmon (known locally as captain fish) and huge grouper, and anglers can spend a day pitting their wits and strength against these denizens of the deep. Onshore angling can be just as much fun, with companies providing equipment and guides so that you can find just the right site for a decent catch. The tidal mangroves make a challenging environment with their constantly changing water levels, and you can even fish directly off the beaches.

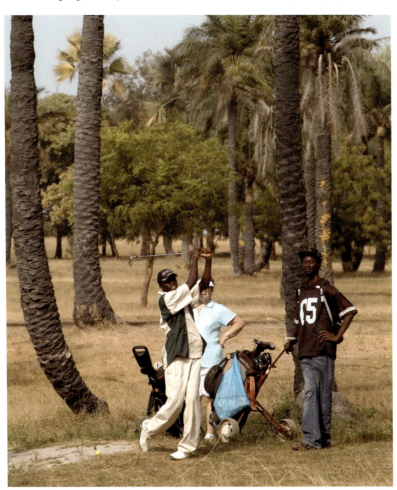

In the rough at Fajara Golf Club

Children

The Gambia makes a great destination for children. It offers a taste of life on the African continent combined with a beach vacation. There are fascinating landscapes and lifestyles to explore, and the warm sunny weather is a constant accompaniment to the daytime activities.

There are very few attractions specifically designed for children in The Gambia. Most young Gambians have few toys and no disposable income of their own. Even a simple football is a much sought-after item, possession of which is something most Gambian children can only dream about. Despite a lack of resources, Gambian children have a natural effervescence that's infectious. Up-country, children from several family compounds usually play together. The environment is totally

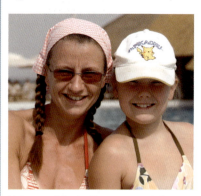

Make sure all the family wears a sun hat

secure as there is always an adult around to keep an eye on the activity. Rolling metal bike rings is a popular pastime, but most of the time children play make-believe or chase games.

Beach fun

The beaches along the tourist coast are soft and fine, so they are perfect for young children who just want to dig or make castles. However, the seas have undercurrents so, although paddling in the shallows is okay, keep swimming for the hotel pool. All the beaches around the major hotels have lifeguards on duty during the day and there is a flag system where the red flag means that sea conditions are not suitable for swimming.

Animal encounters

Animal encounters are among the most enjoyable things about a trip to The Gambia. A visit to Abuko Nature Reserve or the monkey park close to the Senegambia Hotel is certain to result in

Join in with the tribal drumming

sightings, with many animals tame enough to take food from your hand (though you should not feed them). Most hotel grounds have a few monkey inhabitants who are habituated to people, and kids just love it.

Older children with an interest in the natural world have a whole host of other fascinating creatures to enjoy. Rock agama lizards scoot and scurry along walls and into undergrowth, praying mantises lie motionless on branches, and birds are fun to watch. The only problem is that children may have more questions than you can answer – there could be a budding naturalist in the family.

The Gambian up-country national parks are less interesting for small children because of the sheer difficulty in getting to the sites and the amount of walking it takes to find the wildlife. It's possible to see hippos on boat trips up-country but it's not guaranteed, so kids need to have a lot of patience to wait for rewards that may not come.

There are larger animal species at the Kanilai Game Park, including impala, wildebeest, ostriches, zebra and rhino. For crocodiles, the sacred pool at Katchikally is a must – this is definitely the closest your children will ever get to a live, fully grown croc.

Folklore performances

The booming of the drums and the colourful costumes of traditional dances will captivate children. The beat is infectious and they'll be among the first to volunteer to have a go if invited.

Jeep safaris

Kids will love travelling around on the old army trucks and getting off-road with all its bumps and bounces. The high vantage point is excellent for children more used to standing well below adult eye level, and they can get a great view of everything that's happening as you travel along. All these trucks have seat belts, so it's wise to make sure that your children are well strapped in when the truck is on the move.

Funfair

There's a small funfair on Bertil Harding Highway where it meets the Senegambia strip. The park has a range of sit-on rides suitable for under tens, and a visit here would certainly keep children happy for an hour or two.

Karting

There's a small karting track on the inland side of Bertil Harding Highway about 6km (3½ miles) from Kololi on the way to the airport. It has 16 karts

Kids are always happy splashing about in the pool

and is open daily. After a ten-minute introductory session groups or families can race each other in competition and there's a café where you can enjoy refreshments.

Want a pen pal?

Gambian children will definitely want to get to know all about children from other parts of the world and your kids might not be used to all the attention. Most Gambian children want someone to write to – to practise their English – and if your children are in the market for a pen pal, it's a great place to find one. The children will have their address (usually a post box in Banjul where post for an extended family arrives, or sometimes a business address where one of the family works) printed on a scrap of paper. This could be one worthwhile and enduring souvenir of the trip.

Practicalities

The tourist hotels are geared up for families and will have high chairs in the restaurant. Restaurants along the coastal strip welcome children, but facilities such as high chairs are rare and child-specific menus are not that common.

One practical problem that parents will find is in pushing pushchairs around. Pavements are rare and those that exist are rutted and have high kerbs. Roadside verges can be uneven and dusty, making progress slow and uncomfortable for child and parent.

Child health

You'll need to take a little extra care with children's health when you visit The Gambia, but there's no need to worry unduly. Speak to your doctor about appropriate malaria prophylaxis for the age of your children and guard against mosquito bites during your trip. Make sure that they wear insect repellent as the sun sets and after dark, and also if you venture into any of the natural areas.

Never underestimate the strength of the sun. Keep a high-factor cream on skin and replace it after swimming. Make sure your child always wears a hat and protects their eyes with sunglasses.

Clean and cover any small cuts to prevent infection, and monitor any insect bites. If a young child develops diarrhoea make sure they drink plenty of liquids and call a doctor. Dehydration is a concern in any hot climate, so make sure your child is drinking regularly.

Children

Finding a penpal isn't difficult!

Essentials

Passports and visas

Citizens of the UK, Ireland, Australia, New Zealand and Canada can enter The Gambia without a visa for trips of under 90 days, provided they have a full passport with at least six months to run from their date of return.

US citizens require a visa that should be obtained before travel from the Embassy of The Gambia.

Arriving

All international flights, both charter and scheduled, arrive at Banjul International Airport, 15km (9 miles) south of the capital by road.

You will need to fill in an arrivals form. This may be given to you on the flight; it will be stamped and kept by the passport official. Most airline ticket prices now include a $10 entry tax (all UK charter companies now include it). If not, you'll need to pay it on arrival to the passport control official.

At the bag collection carousel you'll be pressured by the luggage porters. They charge a fixed £1 or $1 for their services but this includes putting your bags through the arrival x-ray machines and clearing them through customs, so it is worth using one to avoid the scrum. Tourist taxis are found outside the terminal building and these operate on a fixed fee basis.

Scheduled carriers to The Gambia include SN Brussels and Air Senegal

International, but prices are incredibly expensive and not generally available on the main travel websites such as Expedia and e-bookers. Much more regular and much cheaper are the charter flights provided by the main package holiday companies including Thomas Cook (*www.thomascook.com*) and First Choice (*www.firstchoice.com*). The Gambia Experience (*www.gambia.co.uk*) is a company with a long relationship with the country, who fly to The Gambia throughout the year – though flights aren't as frequent between May and October.

Departing

There are no departure taxes to be paid when you leave The Gambia but you must fill in a departure form, which will be stamped and kept by the passport official.

Credit and debit cards

Credit and debit cards are not widely used. Most restaurants and shops operate on a cash-only basis except in the large hotels and for booking tours. There are ATMs on the Senegambia strip, on Nelson Mandela Street in Banjul and in the Shell petrol station on Kairaba Avenue, all of which are usually empty. You can exchange cash and traveller's cheques at hotels, banks and commercial bureaus in the tourist areas. Cash is easier to exchange and you'll get a better rate of exchange than for traveller's cheques; however, if you lose your cheques or have them stolen, you can get replacements.

Up-country, exchange opportunities are scarce, so it is wise to carry enough dalasis for your needs.

Customs

The following items can be carried into The Gambia without incurring duty.
200 cigarettes or 50 cigars or 150g of tobacco
1 litre of spirits
1 litre of wine or beer
Goods to the value of D1,000

Electricity

The Gambia operates on a 220v AC system. Electric sockets are a mixture of European-style 2-pin and UK-style 3-pin varieties. Electricity supplies are poor and overstretched and you will encounter regular power cuts. It might be practical to pack a torch or some candles and matches.

Email and internet

You'll find internet cafés with cheap access in all towns. Some hotels will have guest internet access (at extra cost).

Green tourist taxis on the Senegambia strip

Language

Each of the ethnic groups in The Gambia has its own language, but Gambians also speak the main language of the region if they are born into a minor ethnic group. The main language of the Kombos is Wolof, while it's Mandinka up-country.

However, the second/third language of every Gambian and the official language of government and the media is English. In the Kombos and tourist areas you'll have no problem making yourself understood if you are an English speaker.

Media

The press in The Gambia is under pressure to keep a pro-government line, and the murder of Deyda Hydara, a leading journalist opposed to President Jammeh, raised the stakes in 2006, though journalists do try to create political debate and discussion. Printed in English, the papers include *The Point* (*www.thepoint.gm*), where Hydara worked, *The Gambia Daily*, *The Independent* and left-wing *Forroyaa*.

Gambia Television has only been broadcasting since 1995 and there is little home-produced programming, but TV news also takes a predominantly pro-government line.

Money

The currency of The Gambia is the dalasi, signified by the letter D or GMD. Dalasi notes come in denominations of 5, 10, 25, 50 and 100 and there are 1 dalasi coins. Each dalasi is made up of 100 bututs, of which the 50 butut coin is the most common. Most other butut coins are no longer used.

In December 2009 The Gambia is due to join the West Africa Monetary Zone, along with Ghana, Guinea, Nigeria and Sierra Leone, so a new currency, the eco, will be introduced to replace the dalasi.

Opening hours

Shops: Monday–Thursday 8am–7pm, Friday–Saturday 8am–noon, with markets open Monday–Saturday all day. Government offices: Monday–Thursday 8am–4pm and Saturday 8am–noon. Tourist restaurants: 8am–midnight if they serve breakfast, otherwise they open around 11am.

Photographing birds by the stream in Kotu

Banks: Monday–Thursday 8am–1pm,
4–6pm, Friday 8–11am.
Post offices: Monday–Thursday
8.20am–12.15pm, 2–4pm, Friday
8.30am–12.15pm, Saturday
8.30am–12.15pm.

Pharmacies

Pharmacies are not widespread in The
Gambia but doctors can also supply
drugs and treatments. If you need
prescription medicines, you should
bring enough for your needs during
your stay. If you need a pharmacy, your
hotel reception or tour rep should be
able to help.

Post

The postal service in The Gambia is
incredibly slow and you'll often arrive
back well before any postcards you may
have sent. The main Government Post
Office (GPO) is Russell Street in Banjul,
close to Albert Market.

Public holidays
Fixed dates
1 January New Year's Day
18 February Independence Day
1 May Labour Day
22 July Revolution Day
15 August Assumption Day
25 December Christmas Day

Moveable dates
March/April Easter Sunday and
Easter Monday
Maolud Nabi: Prophet Mohammed's
birthday

Koriteh: the feast that marks the end
of Ramadan
Tobaski: the feast of the sacrifice
coinciding with the Hajj pilgrimage
to Mecca

Most businesses are also closed on
the first Saturday morning of every
month for Clean the Nation Day, when
neighbourhoods get together to clean a
communal area of litter.

Suggested reading

The following titles are recommended
to help you understand the background
to the development of The Gambia as a
political entity and a multifaceted
society. There are also books to help
you to identify the animals and birds
you spot when there.
*Field Guide to the Birds of The Gambia
and Senegal* Clive Barlow (RSPB/Yale
University Press). The birdwatchers'
'bible', with pages of pictures, and field
notes on habits and diet.

*Common Reptiles of The Gambia,
Common Mammals of The Gambia*
and *Common Amphibians of The
Gambia* Linda Barnett and Craig
Emms (Darwin Field Centre for
Biodiversity Research). These three
booklet guides, aimed at the interested
amateur, have useful information with
excellent photography that will help
you identify animals you come across
on your travels.

Forest Dwellers Stella Brewer
(Collins). The story of Brewer's fight
to save and rehabilitate the chimps at
the Gambia River National Park.

Roots: The Saga of an American Family Alex Haley (Doubleday). The story of Haley's family tree, traced from Kunte Kinte of Juffureh, Gambia, taken into slavery and sold in America, through the generations to author Alex Haley.

Under the Baobab Tree Rosemary Long (Orion). A Scottish woman married to a Gambian is trying to make a success of running a guesthouse in the country in the 1990s.

The Rough Guide to World Music: Africa and the Middle East Simon Broughton et al. (Rough Guides). A detailed explanation and discussion of West African music and its influence on modern 'world music'.

Historical Dictionary of The Gambia Arnold Hughes and Harry Gailey (Scarecrow Press). Hughes was director of the Centre of West African Studies and Gailey is professor of African Studies at San Jose University, both eminently qualified to lead the reader through the intricacies of the history of The Gambia.

Griot and Griottes: Masters of World and Music Thomas A. Hale (Indiana University Press). Fascinating book about the role of musicians and storytellers in West African society.

Telephones

Telecommunications are provided in the main by Gamtel. Most hotels provide international direct dialling but mark-ups are high. The alternatives are to buy a calling card from Gamtel offices (there is one in every town), or make a call from a Gamtel office and pay at the end of your call. Mobile provision is good along the coastal strip and Gamtel and Africell have connections with the major call companies (check with your provider before leaving home). Roaming charges are high and it may be more cost-effective to buy a Gambian SIM card (at a Gamtel office) and use that during your stay.

The international code for The Gambia is 220 followed by a seven-figure number.

Time

The Gambia operates in the same time zone as Greenwich Mean Time, which means noon in Banjul is noon

Horseriding along Kotu beach at sunset

in London (October to March) and Cape Town, 7am in New York and Toronto, 10pm in Sydney and midnight in Wellington.

Toilets

Public toilets are nonexistent in The Gambia. You'll need to visit facilities in cafés, tourist attractions and hotels. Toilets in international establishments should be European style. At local cafés, toilet rolls may not be available, so always carry some just in case.

When travelling up-country and in the national parks there are no public toilets. In an emergency you'll need to take refuge behind a verdant bush – but check for snakes first.

Travellers with disabilities

There are few aids for people with disabilities in The Gambia. Some hotels are built on a single storey but few have rooms designed specifically for disabled travellers. Getting around isn't easy on dirt tracks and uneven pavements; however, there will always be someone willing to help in difficult situations. There is no adapted public transport and disabled visitors should get the advice of a travel agent or tour operator before booking.

For more holiday and travel information for people with disabilities contact:
Holiday Care Services
Tel: 0845 124 9971 (UK)
www.holidaycare.org.uk

CONVERSION TABLE

FROM	TO	MULTIPLY BY
Inches	Centimetres	2.54
Feet	Metres	0.3048
Yards	Metres	0.9144
Miles	Kilometres	1.6090
Acres	Hectares	0.4047
Gallons	Litres	4.5460
Ounces	Grams	28.35
Pounds	Grams	453.6
Pounds	Kilograms	0.4536
Tons	Tonnes	1.0160

To convert back, for example from centimetres to inches, divide by the number in the third column.

MEN'S SUITS

UK	36	38	40	42	44	46	48
Rest of Europe	46	48	50	52	54	56	58
USA	36	38	40	42	44	46	48

DRESS SIZES

UK	8	10	12	14	16	18
France	36	38	40	42	44	46
Italy	38	40	42	44	46	48
Rest of Europe	34	36	38	40	42	44
USA	6	8	10	12	14	16

MEN'S SHIRTS

UK	14	14.5	15	15.5	16	16.5	17
Rest of Europe	36	37	38	39/40	41	42	43
USA	14	14.5	15	15.5	16	16.5	17

MEN'S SHOES

UK	7	7.5	8.5	9.5	10.5	11
Rest of Europe	41	42	43	44	45	46
USA	8	8.5	9.5	10.5	11.5	12

WOMEN'S SHOES

UK	4.5	5	5.5	6	6.5	7
Rest of Europe		38	38	39	39	40	41
USA		6	6.5	7	7.5	8	8.5

Emergencies

Emergency numbers

Ambulance *16*

Police *17*

Fire Service *18*

Health risks

The authorities don't have any vaccination requirements unless you are arriving from an area infected with yellow fever. If you intend to spend most of your time on the beach and around the pool, you won't need vaccinations, but if you are planning to spend any time up-country in the villages or travelling long distances on public transport then it would be wise to plan a vaccination programme with your doctor. Ensure that your meningitis, polio, yellow fever, typhoid, tetanus and Hepatitis A needs are discussed. It's important to state that the risk of these diseases throughout The Gambia is low, but some pockets still exist and outbreaks occur in other parts of Africa; so it's better to be safe.

A much more potent risk in The Gambia, however, is malaria, a potentially fatal disease carried by mosquitoes. The disease is passed to humans through the bite of an infected insect, and the most effective way to reduce risk is not to get bitten in the first place. Cover up exposed skin, especially around sunset and through the night, use insect spray or cream on your skin and put insecticide in your room (either spray or light a coil). If mosquitoes are present in the bedroom, sleep under a mosquito net.

Anti-malaria medication – prophylactic tablets – offer protection against the disease. These come in several types, each with a particular regime and some possible side effects, so getting advice from your doctor is of paramount importance. Always take the tablets as instructed to ensure maximum protection.

Any course of prophylactic tablets is not 100 per cent effective, so it is important that, if you have flu-like symptoms anytime up to a year after returning from The Gambia, you visit your doctor and have a blood test, to rule out malaria as the cause.

Most travellers find that an upset stomach is the worst they suffer while in The Gambia. This can easily be caused by a change in diet or too much sun and usually improves with a day of no solid food and plenty of fluids.

Health care

Health-care provision is not widespread in The Gambia; the system is under-funded and lacks much of the specialist equipment found in hospitals in Europe and North America.

The main hospital is the Royal Victoria Teaching Hospital (*tel: 422 3756*) on Independence Drive in Banjul, and there is a new hospital at

Farrafenni. Smaller towns have local clinics, but these have few resources.

Private clinics in the tourist area include: The Lamtoro Clinic (*tel: 446 0934*) on the Senegambia strip, and the Westfield Clinic (*tel: 439 2213*), Westfields Road, Serrekunda.

Carrying a small collection of basic medicines such as paracetamol/aspirin and anti-diarrhoea tablets should see you through the most common health problems.

Insurance

Having adequate insurance cover is vital. The Gambia has no reciprocal health agreements with other countries and visitors will have to pay for any treatment they need. Travellers should ensure that they have cover for private treatment of illness or injury and cover for repatriation back to their homeland should the situation warrant it.

Travellers should always have cover for everything they carry with them in case of loss or theft.

Insurance companies also usually provide cover for cancellation or travel delay in their policies. Though not essential cover, this offers some compensation if travel plans go awry.

Crime and scams

There are no major problems with crime in The Gambia; however, petty crime such as theft is a growing problem in the tourist area. Don't carry large amounts of cash or flaunt expensive items. Keep money etc. in a secure interior pocket and lock valuables in the hotel safe.

Begging and 'bumstering' are an irritation more than a danger, and the amounts of money requested are generally small.

Embassies

Australia Australian High Commission, *2 Second Rangoon Close, Accra, Ghana. Tel: 233 21 701 2961-3 or 233 21 777 080*
Canada The Canadian Embassy, *PO Box 3373, Dakar, Senegal. Tel: (221) 889-4700.*
New Zealand High Commission of New Zealand, *Block C (2nd floor), Hatfield Gardens, 1110 Arcadia Street, Private Bag X17, Hatfield, Pretoria 0028, South Africa. Tel: (27 12) 342 8656.*
South Africa South African Embassy, *PO Box 21010, Dakar, Senegal. Tel: (221) 865-1959.*
UK British High Commission, *48 Atlantic Road, Fajara (PO Box 507), Banjul. Tel: 449 5133.*
US Embassy of the United States, *Kairaba Avenue, Fajara (PMB 19), Banjul. Tel: 439 2856.*

Police

The police in The Gambia have a reasonable reputation, better than most in Africa. Make sure you carry identification and papers for your vehicle if you are driving. Tourist police patrol the resorts and popular beaches mainly to keep control of bumsters. Police Headquarters, *Ecowas Avenue, Banjul. Tel: 422 7222.*

Directory

Accommodation star ratings

Most hotels in The Gambia price rooms in a major foreign currency, usually either pounds sterling or euros. The price guide here (per room) has taken current pricing and converted it to dalasi (approximately 50 dalasi to the pound sterling), but prices may vary due to fluctuating exchange rates.

The up-country lodges are priced very differently from hotels along the southwest coast, and most fall into the lowest quartile of the one-star price bracket.

★	under 1,500 dalasi
★★	1,500–3,000 dalasi
★★★	3,000–4,000 dalasi
★★★★	over 4,000 dalasi

Eating out price range

There's a big price difference between local eateries and the restaurants that serve the tourist coast, so price ranges here concentrate on helping you decide which are inexpensive or expensive tourist-oriented places to eat.

Prices are for a three-course dinner for one without drinks.

★	under 300 dalasi
★★	300–750 dalasi
★★★	750–1,000 dalasi
★★★★	over 1,000 dalasi

BANJUL

ACCOMMODATION

Denton's Beach Resort ★

Right on the beach at Denton Bridge with the best range of watersports (fishing, wave riders and kayaks) on the doorstep. The three lodges and four rooms mean it's a cosy place to stay. There's a seafood restaurant on-site but very little else in the immediate vicinity, so you'd need a taxi or car if you wanted to venture out.

Denton Bridge, Banjul. Tel: 777 4777.

Palm Grove Hotel ★★

Set on the west side of Denton Bridge heading towards the south-coast resorts, the Palm Grove is a comfortable place to stay but a little caught between two areas. Rooms are a good size and there's a good beach and large pool. Just be prepared to taxi if you want to do anything outside the hotel.

Banjul Highway, Banjul. Tel: 420 1620. www.palmgrovehotel-gambia.com

Corinthia Atlantic Hotel ★★★★

The most luxurious hotel in the capital, the Corinthia Atlantic Hotel is a favourite with business travellers to The Gambia but also has good leisure facilities including a good-sized pool, a spa and a sandy beach, and the grounds are well kept. It's just a couple of minutes' walk into the heart of Banjul but nightlife in the capital is limited so not really recommended for nightowls.

Marina Parade, Banjul.
Tel: 422 8601.
www.corinthiahotels.com

EATING OUT
Al-Samadeh Refreshment Centre ★
A simple beach bar, but a great place for a cooling drink after visiting the market. It's just by the fish landing station and you can watch all the activity of the ferries and boats coming and going.
On the beach, Banjul. Tel: 422 9354. Open: Mon–Sat 9am–7pm.

Michel's Seafood Restaurant ★★
One of the few formal restaurants in the capital, Michel's draws the ex-pats and civil servants from the government offices. It's a good option if you don't want a simple snack.
29 Independence Drive, Banjul. Tel: 422 3108. Open: Mon–Sat 11am–3pm, 6–9pm.

ENTERTAINMENT
Nightclub
The Corinthia Atlantic Hotel is one of the few places with activities after dark and attracts tourists, expats and Gambians in the evenings. It's at its busiest at weekends.
Corinthia Atlantic Hotel, Marina Parade, Banjul. Tel: 422 8601. www.corinthiahotels.com

SPORT AND LEISURE
Denton Bridge Watersports
Organises deep-sea, sport fishing trips and rental kayaks and wave runners for inshore exploration.
Denton Bridge, Banjul. Tel: 777 3777.

Gamtours
The largest and longest-established ground tour operator in the country. Has a full range of day tours and can book trips and attractions around the country.
PO Box 101, Banjul. Tel: 439 1479. www.gamtours.gm

Mamadou W. Barry
Well-qualified and personable bird guide, Mamadou has eyes like a hawk.
30A Grant Street, Banjul. Tel: 992 8882. snipe8882@yahoo.com

Vitala Spa
A well-equipped day spa with massage and facial facilities.
Corinthia Atlantic Hotel, Marine Parade, Banjul. Tel: 422 8601.

SERREKUNDA AND THE TOURIST COAST
ACCOMMODATION
Sukuta Camping ★
This German-owned campsite is well known by those travelling on the trans-Africa trails, arriving overland from Mauritania to the north or from the centre of the continent. Prices are incredibly inexpensive both for a site or for a bungalow, and there's a restaurant on-site. The owners have lots of experience of independent travelling in Africa and are a mine of good advice.
Bijilo Road, Sukuta. Tel: 991 7786. www.campingsukuta.de

African Village Hotel ★–★★
This small budget hotel gets lots of repeat visitors for its location close to Cape Point and its good

food. The rooms are designed like African round huts – hence the hotel name – and are basic but clean, and there's a pool and beach access. Could do with a bit of sprucing up, though.

98 Atlantic Road, Bakau. Tel: 449 5384. www.africanvillagehotel. gm

Palm Beach Hotel ★★

The rooms of the Palm Beach are spacious and clean, though some of the fittings are a little worn. The hotel sits on a wonderful stretch of beach, with sun beds sheltered by mature palms. Blocks of rooms are divided by narrow alleys bedecked with flowers and trees, which can make the lower rooms quite dark. Ask for an upper room or a room facing out of the resort if you'd prefer more light. Each room has a small balcony or patio and the hotel has a reasonable-sized pool and a restaurant.

Off Kotu Stream Road, Kotu. Tel: 446 2111.

Safari Garden Hotel ★★

Excellent, small Gambian-owned hotel with pretty, bright rooms, each with a spacious patio, and there's a small communal pool set in a private courtyard. There's a restaurant on-site and activities such as batik, yoga and drumming. The hotel is a member of the Association of Small-Scale Enterprises in Tourism and is keen to encourage fair trade and sustainability.

Off Atlantic Road, Fajara. Tel: 449 5887. www.safarigarden.com

Bakotu Hotel ★★★

Set on the landward side of Kotu Stream Road, the lack of direct access to the beach is the only disadvantage of this well-designed resort, with The Captain's Table gourmet restaurant on-site. Rooms are well furnished for the price, and there's a small pool area and guest laundry facilities. Some rooms overlook the stream with its wealth of birdlife. It's only a couple of minutes to a range of restaurants

and to Kotu beach itself.

2 Kotu Stream Road, Kotu. Tel: 446 5555. www.bakotuhotel.com

Ngala Lodge ★★★

This European-owned small lodge has grown out of the ruin of an old ambassador's mansion. Ngala has a range of individually furnished rooms, from tower suites to luxury African bungalows, all set in verdant tropical gardens and overlooking the ocean. The restaurant is excellent (*see p153*).

64 Atlantic Boulevard, Fajara. Tel: 449 4045. www.ngalalodge.com (packages booked through The Gambia Experience www.gambia.co.uk).

Omakan Hotel ★★★

A brand-new lodge hotel opened in late 2006, the Omakan is a Gambian-owned and European-managed boutique property fitted and decorated to a high standard. Accommodation is made up of good-sized rooms and spacious bungalows set around a pretty plunge pool. There's a nice bar and a good

restaurant on-site (food can be served in your suite or bungalow). It's quiet and secluded for those who want a personal retreat.
Sukuta Village. Tel: 446 6442. www.omakanhotel.com

Senegambia Beach Hotel ★★★
This large resort has been a long-standing favourite for many years and continues to impress with a good standard of accommodation and communal space, even if some of the design elements look a little bit dated. The gardens are spacious, there's a good-sized pool, tennis courts and spa – a little something for all the family, plus the restaurants and bars of the Senegambia strip just outside the door. There's even a resident bird specialist who'll give you a tour of the grounds.
Senegambia Road, Kololi. Tel: 466 2717. www. senegambiahotel.com

Sunbeach Hotel ★★★
A pretty, low-rise resort of 184 rooms and suites right at the tip of Cape

Point, with spacious accommodation, generous patios and garden areas, some with sea views. The furniture is bright, with colourful fabrics mixed with rattan and bamboo. The hotel features three restaurants, including a buffet venue and a pizza parlour, and has a good-sized pool, so it's a great family option. The beach here curves around the point, offering a picturesque vista.
Kofi Annan Street, Cape Point, Bakau. Tel: 449 7190. www.sunbeachhotel.com

Coconut Residence ★★★–★★★★
A beautifully designed and furnished tropical lodge, Coconut Residence sets itself apart from others in its class with luxurious modern touches and a sophisticated ambience. The rooms can't be faulted and there's a gourmet restaurant, plunge pool and lush landscaped gardens. Perhaps the only disadvantage is that it doesn't have beach access, and the

atmosphere favours adults rather than families.
Kerr Serign, Serrekunda. Tel: 446 3377. www. coconutresidence.com

Kairaba Beach Hotel ★★★★
A sympathetically designed four-star hotel set at the beach end of the Senegambia strip, the Kairaba has spacious and elegantly designed tropical rooms set in verdant gardens and fronting onto a large, free-form pool. Standard rooms are set on the land-side of the reception area opposite the hotel offices so their location isn't as good as more deluxe room options.
Senegambia Road, Kololi. Tel: 461 2940. www.kairabahotel.com

Mandina Lodge ★★★★
Award-winning eco-lodge with luxury rooms floating on the *bolong* or surrounded by the jungle. The Lodge has less than a dozen detached suites, some floating on the water of Mandina Bolong, or others set in the sacred

forest itself. This is a place to seriously chill out rather than for those wanting a fast-paced beach break.

Makasutu Cultural Forest, Mandina Ba. Tel: 990 0268. www.makasutu.com

Ocean Bay ★★★★

A well-designed, recent addition on Cape Point, the low-rise Ocean Bay features spacious rooms with well-proportioned dark wood furnishings and good-sized patio or balcony. There are several restaurants on site, a pool, kids' pool and a range of sports. There's also a kids' club.

Kofi Annan Street, Cape Point, Bakau. Tel: 449 4265. www.oceanbayhotel.com

Sheraton Gambia Hotel, Resort and Spa ★★★★

This beautifully styled African adobe resort opens its doors as this book is published and it is the first luxury spa resort in The Gambia. The whole resort is exquisitely designed with modern Afro-Asian furnishings and design elements set in adobe-style, mud-walled, low-rise buildings. The 195 rooms are cool and elegant in neutral tones embellished by the warmth of hardwood accents. There is an all-day dining restaurant and a fusion evening-only dining option.

Brufut Heights, AU Highway, Serrekunda. Tel: 441 0878. www.starwoodhotels.com

EATING OUT

Boss Lady ★★

A great African restaurant where you can try Gambian staples including tasting *domoda*, *benachin* and *yassa*. No alcohol.

Kotu Beach. No phone. Open: daily 5–11pm.

Kunte Kinte Bar ★★

On the southern side of Kotu Stream. Kunte Kinte is a beach bar with snacks and main meals served throughout the day and into the evening. Unpretentious but tasty good-value food, particularly the Wednesday and Sunday barbecues.

Kotu Beach. Tel: 990 1283. Open: daily 9am–midnight.

Al Basha Lebanese Restaurant ★★★

Excellent Lebanese *mezze* (collection of small dishes that make up a full meal) and grilled meats. The décor will certainly get you in the mood for Eastern promise.

Senegambia Road, Kololi. Tel: 446 3300. Open: daily 7pm–midnight.

Weezo's ★★★

One of The Gambia's coolest venues, Weezo's has the only genuine Mexican food with great hot and spicy enchiladas and fajitas, or choose modern European dishes including great tapas. The food doesn't disappoint.

132 Kairaba Avenue, Fajara. Tel: 449 6918. www.weezos.co.uk. Open: daily 5pm–1am.

The Butcher's Shop ★★★★

Every expat knows where The Butcher's Shop is – it's been supplying excellent organic and free-range meat since 1993, and has expanded into a delicatessen. Only later did the owners develop the restaurant, but it's now one of the best smart eateries in the country. Breakfast and lunches see excellent pastries, sandwiches and fresh fruit juices. Sumptuous meat dishes pad out salads and Mediterranean dishes at dinner. It's expensive but excellent.

130 Kairaba Avenue, Fajara. Tel: 449 5069. www.thebutchersshop gambia.com Open: Mon–Sat 8am–late.

The Captain's Table ★★★★

The menu at this gourmet restaurant changes with the seasons, as only local organic ingredients make the grade, but meat always includes the excellent local Ndama beef fillet. A range of international dishes mix with Asian and Arab suggestions. The restaurant is nicely designed and service is attentive.

Kotu Village. Tel: 446 6111. Open: noon–11pm.

Ngala Lodge ★★★★

If you don't stay at the Ngala Lodge, it's worth booking a table at the restaurant and dressing up for the best European food in The Gambia. There's live music in the background and a decent wine list. Worth pushing the boat out for.

64 Atlantic Boulevard, Bakau. Tel: 449 7672. Open: Mon–Sat 7–10pm.

Shikra ★★★★

The Kairaba Hotel's fine-dining option is a beautifully designed Asian restaurant concentrating on Thai dishes but with delicate sushi and some Chinese options. There's also a choice of vegetarian offerings.

Kairaba Hotel, Senegambia Road, Kololi. Tel: 446 2940. Open: Mon–Sat 7–11pm.

ENTERTAINMENT

Aquarius Café

One of the latest lounge/clubs that offers a different style of music each night. There's always a good crowd during the tourist season.

Kololi Casino Complex, Senegambia. Tel: 446 0247. Open: daily 6pm–5am.

Churchill's

A long-standing favourite British-owned bar that has popular karaoke evenings on Wednesday, Thursday and Saturday, and live Premiership matches for the boys.

Palma Rima Road, Kotu. Tel: 990 3383. Open: daily 11am–1am.

Dunes Casino

You can enjoy slots and table games at this small casino.

Kotu Beach Point. Tel: 446 5660. Open: Mon–Sat 4pm–5am.

Jazziz

Currently one of the places to be seen. It's a great place for a drink early evening, then later you've got music and live acts at weekends. A good mixed crowd adds to the atmosphere.

Palma Rima Road, Kotu. Tel: 446 2175. Open: daily 5pm–5am.

Jokor

The most famous *mbalax* club in The Gambia, Jokor throbs with great music at weekends and hosts fantastic live concerts. During the week there's a different

sound every evening. It's a great place to meet locals.
Westfield Junction.
Tel: 992 2555.
Open: nightly midnight–5am.

Seaview Bar
A great terrace with views over the beach, this is a good vantage point for a sunset drink or later when there is live entertainment.
Off Bertil Harding Highway near the Senegambia Hotel, Kololi. Tel: 998 7214. Open: daily 11am–2am.

Sinatra's
This bar has a sunny terrace where you can enjoy a drink after visiting the craft market, and a range of snacks and main dishes if you find yourself hungry.
Banjul Road, Bakau. Tel: 449 5034. Open: Mon–Sat 11am–11pm.

Weezo's
After a fantastic meal of tapas or Mexican food, stay at Weezo's for a late-night music lounge atmosphere, or disco night when Euro-pop blares over the speakers.

131 Kairaba Avenue, Fajara. Tel: 779 0001. Open: daily 6pm–2am.

Wow Nightclub
Small joint playing a mixture of disco, *reggae* and rap, it's popular with tourists and locals.
Senegambia Road, Kololi. Tel: 446 0668. Open: daily midnight–5am.

SPORT AND LEISURE

Bird Guide Association
This bone-fide organisation has a hut next to Kotu Stream and you can contract a guide to show you the best sports in the area.
Kotu Bridge, Kotu Stream Road, Kotu. Tel: 998 2234.

Camel Safari
Treks down Tanje beach on the back of a dromedary.
Coast Road, Tanje Village. Tel: 446 1083.

D&D Buggy's and Bikes
Rents bikes, scooters and quads by the hour, day or longer. Daily rates are fixed, but longer rentals are negotiable.
Kofi Annan Road, Cape Point, Bakau. Tel: 771 9756.

Darboes Bicycle Hire/Rental Service
Bicycle rental by the hour or the day.
Kotu Stream Road (opposite the Badala Hotel). Tel: 770 1587.

Fajara Club
Has The Gambia's best golf course (over 16s only), and facilities for a range of other sports.
Off Atlantic Road, Fajara. Tel: 449 5457.

Jane's Boats
Morning and afternoon trips around Tanbi Wetlands and expeditions upriver on neatly kept double-decker pirogues.
PO Box 4414, Bakau. Tel: 776 8074.

Vitala Spa
Independent spas operating in three hotels on the tourist strip. You can enjoy massage, aromatherapy and other beauty treatments.
Kairaba Hotel (also at the Ocean Bay Hotel and the Sunbeach Hotel), Senegambia Road, Kololi. Tel: 446 2940.

SHOPPING
Craft markets or *bengdulas* are found in

the following locations in the Kombos:
Cape Point – between the Sun Beach and Ocean Bay Hotels.
Bakau – opposite the African Village Hotel.
Fajara – on the beach opposite Hotel Fajara.
Kotu – between the Kombo Beach and Bungalow Beach Hotels.
Kololi – at the top of Senegambia Road.
Brikama – opposite the police station.

Lemonfish Art Gallery
Arts workshop with almost 30 local artists displaying work. Gift shop with other crafts on sale.
Kartong Village.
Tel: 439 4586.

Nyamu's Gift Shop
This gift shop upstairs in the reception area sells the best selection of books and maps along the coast, plus a range of tropical clothing, gifts and handicrafts.
Senegambia Beach Hotel, Senegambia Road, Kololi.
Tel: 446 2717.

JANJANGBUREH AND THE MID RIVER REGION
ACCOMMODATION
Baobolong Camp ★
A cluster of round huts set around a communal courtyard, this is a basic but clean option with friendly staff.
Owen Street, Janjangbureh.
Tel: 567 6133.

Bird Safari Camp ★
Set on the water's edge, this nature camp sits east of Janjangbureh town. Accommodation is a mixture of 'Out of Africa' safari tents and round huts and it's surrounded by riverine forest. A small pool adds a touch of luxury.
1.5km (1 mile) north of Janjangbureh, McCarthy Island. Tel: 567 6108 (office in Janjangbureh).
www.bsc.gm

Janjangbureh Camp ★
Set on the riverbank north of the island, Janjangbureh Camp has nicely designed rustic rooms and a good restaurant serving Gambian dishes. There's no electricity, so it's very peaceful and the

property is lit at night by romantic kerosene lamps. There are free boat transfers into town.
North Shore, opposite McCarthy Island, Janjangbureh. Tel: 449 4360 (company office in Bakau).
www.gambiariver.com

Tendaba Camp ★
Originally built to cater to hunters, this riverside lodge now attracts wildlife watchers, photographers and twitchers from around the world. It's a great place to pick up a guide, and it runs several excursions to Kiang West and Bao Bolong national parks. Simple rooms, but there's a restaurant, pool and a great bar overlooking the river.
Tendaba Village, Kwinella. Tel: 554 1024.

Sindola Safari Lodge ★★–★★★
The most luxurious up-country game lodge, with abundant grounds and spacious traditional-style lodges, games room and pool. There are wonderful little touches of Africa, like the giant wooden chess set carved

into traditional figures and animals.

Kanilai Village.
Tel: 448 3415.

Chimp Rehabilitation Visitor Camp ★★★★

Wilderness tented camp in the heart of the national park where you can spend time with the project workers on the Chimpanzee Rehabilitation Project. Full board included in the price, but much of the money goes into project funds.

River Gambia National Park (book accommodation through Hidden Gambia. Tel: (UK) 01527 576239. www.hiddengambia.com).

EATING OUT

Janjangbureh Lodge ★

The best food in Janjangbureh, served in a round hut-style restaurant with outside adobe-style tables on the riverside. It is one of the few places up-country where you have a choice of a range of vegetarian dishes. Book ahead if you can, especially if you aren't staying at the lodge. There's a

boat transfer from Janjangbureh to the north bank across the river.

North Shore, opposite McCarthy Island, Janjangbureh. Tel: 449 4360 (company office in Bakau). www.gambiariver.com. Open: daily 7–9pm (book ahead).

Tendaba Camp ★

There's a good range of Gambian food and international meals and snacks at the restaurant here. Nothing fancy, but it makes a change to be able to order something different from the standard buffet fare served in most lodges.

Tendaba Village, Kwinella. Tel: 554 1024. Open: daily 7am–10pm.

Sindola Lodge ★–★★

The best up-country option, with excellent Gambian and international dishes served in a rustic, bush-style building in the midst of the tropical gardens.

Kanilai. Tel: 448 3415. Open: daily 8–10am, 11am–3pm, 7–9pm.

ENTERTAINMENT

Riverside bar

The wooden bar on a jetty over the river shallows is one of the prettiest places in The Gambia to enjoy a cold Julbrew at sunset and listen to the frogs after dark.

Tendaba Camp, Tendaba Village, Kwinella. Tel: 554 1024. Open: daily 5–11pm.

Folkloric show

If the camps at Janjangbureh are full or have big groups, the owners will usually arrange for a dancing and drumming performance during the evening. Enquire whether the lodge you book will have entertainment or ring ahead to Baobolong Camp, Bird Safari Camp or Janjangbureh Camp, for details if you aren't a guest but want to watch.

SPORT AND LEISURE

Batik course

Janjangbureh Camp runs batik courses (must be pre-booked) so you can learn about the techniques and produce

your own African-
inspired patterns.
North Shore, opposite
McCarthy Island,
Janjangbureh.
Tel: 449 4360 (company
office in Bakau).
www.gambiariver.com
Birdwatching
Bird Safari Camp
offers guided cross-
country and river
birdwatching safaris.
1.5km (1 mile) north of
Janjangbureh, McCarthy
Island. Tel: 567 6108
(office in Janjangbureh).
www.bsc.gm
Tendaba Camp is a
centre of excellence for
birdwatching and has a
pool of guides for you to
hire who are highly
experienced in wildlife
and bird tracking. The
camp also runs regular
boat trips to Kiang West
and Bao Bolong parks,
either for groups or for
independent travellers.
Tendaba Village,
Kwinella. Tel: 554 1024.
Drumming lessons
Bird Safari Camp
organises regular
drumming courses for
beginners and improvers
(also Janjangbureh
Camp, details above).

1.5km (1 mile) north of
Janjangbureh, McCarthy
Island. Tel: 567 6108
(office in Janjangbureh).
www.bsc.gm
Kayaking
Janjangbureh Camp
has kayaks for hire so
you can explore the
river up and down
stream.
North Shore, opposite
McCarthy Island,
Janjangbureh.
Tel: 449 4360 (company
office in Bakau).
www.gambiariver.com

SHOPPING

Lumos (country markets)
take place in Farafenni
on Sundays and in Koto
on Mondays.

Index

Acknowledgements

Thomas Cook wishes to thank the photographer, PETE BENNETT, for the loan of the photographs reproduced in this book, to whom copyright in the photographs belongs, except the following:
PICTURES COLOUR LIBRARY 75, 111
WIKIMEDIA COMMONS 45 (KG), 76
WORLD PICTURES 1

The author and photographer would like to thank Batch S Fye for his logistical help during research for the book and Mandi Watson for her unending enthusiasm, support and friendship.

Copy-editing: LYNN BRESLER for CAMBRIDGE PUBLISHING MANAGEMENT LTD

Index: KAROLIN THOMAS for CAMBRIDGE PUBLISHING MANAGEMENT LTD

Maps: PC GRAPHICS, Old Woking, UK

Proofreading: JAN McCANN for CAMBRIDGE PUBLISHING MANAGEMENT LTD

SEND YOUR THOUGHTS TO
BOOKS@THOMASCOOK.COM

We're committed to providing the very best up-to-date information in our travel guides and constantly strive to make them as useful as they can be. You can help us to improve future editions by letting us have your feedback. If you've made a wonderful discovery on your travels that we don't already feature, if you'd like to inform us about recent changes to anything that we do include, or if you simply want to let us know your thoughts about this guidebook and how we can make it even better – we'd love to hear from you.

Send us ideas, discoveries and recommendations today and then look out for your valuable input in the next edition of this title. And, as an extra 'thank you' from Thomas Cook Publishing, you'll be automatically entered into our exciting prize draw.

Emails to the above address, or letters to Travellers Project Editor, Thomas Cook Publishing, PO Box 227, Coningsby Road, Peterborough PE3 8SB, UK.

Please don't forget to let us know which title your feedback refers to!